*The Routledge Anthology of*

# CROSS-GENDERED VERSE

*The Routledge Anthology of Cross-Gendered Verse* is a thoroughly unique collection of poems which cross the permeable lines of gender.

Over the centuries many poets have explored the possibilities, personae and power of assuming the voice of the opposite gender – from Geoffrey Chaucer writing as the Wife of Bath to Anne Sexton writing as Jesus, with a very broad spectrum in between. By gathering these poems into *The Routledge Anthology of Cross-Gendered Verse*, editors Alan Michael Parker and Mark Willhardt shed a whole new light on poetry and poetical discourse.

This fascinating anthology:

- spans seven centuries of cross-gendered verse
- incorporates the work of both canonical and lesser-known poets
- includes a substantial introduction which presents an historical, literary, social and theoretical context
- provides an extensive bibliography of further reading.

*The Routledge Anthology of Cross-Gendered Verse* will be a delightful and intriguing addition to the bookshelves of any poetry lover. It is valuable reading to anyone interested in issues of gender, masks and voices: from literary studies and creative writing to gender and performance studies.

**Alan Michael Parker** is a poet whose work has appeared in publications such as the *New Republic, New Yorker* and *Paris Review*. He is also a regular book reviewer for the *New Yorker*, and Contributing Editor at *Boulevard* magazine. He is Assistant Professor of English and Creative Writing at Penn State Erie, The Behrend College.

**Mark Willhardt** is a Visiting Assistant Professor of English at the University of St. Thomas. He is presently preparing his manuscript *Hugh MacDiarmid and the Contradictions of Nation* for publication.

*The Routledge Anthology of*

# CROSS-GENDERED VERSE

*Edited by*
ALAN MICHAEL PARKER AND
MARK WILLHARDT

LONDON AND NEW YORK

First published 1996
by Routledge
11 New Fetter Lane, London EC4P 4EE

Transferred to Digital Printing 2004

Simultaneously published in the USA and Canada
by Routledge
29 West 35th Street, New York, NY 10001

Typeset in Janson by
Florencetype Ltd, Stoodleigh, Devon

*British Library Cataloguing in Publication Data*
A catalogue record for this book is available from
the British Library

*Library of Congress Cataloguing in Publication Data*

The Routledge Anthology of Cross-Gendered Verse
edited by Alan Michael Parker and Mark Willhardt.
p. cm
Includes bibliographical references (p. ).
1. English poetry. 2. Women–Poetry.
3. Masculinity (Psychology)–Poetry.
4. Femininity (Psychology)–Poetry. 5. Point of view (Literature)
6. Persona (Literature) 7. American poetry. 8. Men–Poetry.
I. Parker, Alan Michael, 1961– . II. Willhardt, Mark, 1965– .
PR1195.W6R68 1996
821.008–dc20                                      95-18991

ISBN 0–415–11290–7 (hbk)
ISBN 0–415–11291–5 (pbk)

For Felicia and Ronda

# Contents

Acknowledgements      xii
Permissions      xiii
Introduction      1

Poetry
GEOFFREY CHAUCER 1340?–1400
  from The Prologe of the Wyves Tale of Bathe      5
WILLIAM DUNBAR 1460?–1520?
  The Tua Mariit Wemen and the Wedo      10
  Translation by Mark Willhardt      13
NICHOLAS BRETON 1545?–1626?
  A Sweet Lullaby      16
SIR WALTER RALEIGH 1552?–1618
  The Nymph's Reply to the Shepherd      18
THOMAS LODGE 1558?–1625
  Rosalind's Madrigal      19
ROBERT GREENE 1560–1592
  The Shepherd's Wife's Song      21
JOHN DONNE 1572–1631
  Sapho To Philaenis      23
MARY SIDNEY WROTH, COUNTESS OF MONTGOMERY
  1586?–1640?
  The Duke's Song      25
ROBERT HERRICK 1591–1674
  The Mad Maid's Song      26
ANDREW MARVELL 1621–1678
  The Nymph Complaining For the Death of Her Fawn      27
JOHN DRYDEN 1631–1700
  Farewell, Ungrateful Traitor      31
APHRA BEHN 1640–1689
  The Dream, from "A Voyage to the Isle of Love"      32

Silvio's Complaint: A Song, To a Fine Scotch Tune     32

ALEXANDER POPE 1688–1744
   Eloisa to Abelard     35

MARY MONCK 1690?–1715
   On A Romantic Lady     45

JUDITH MADAN 1702–1781
   Abelard to Eloisa     46

MARY LEAPOR 1722–1746
   Strephon to Celia. A Modern Love-Letter     51

WILLIAM BLAKE 1757–1827
   Nurse's Song     53
   The Angel     53
   Song (My silks and fine array . . .)     54

JEAN GLOVER 1758–1801
   O'er the Muir Amang the Heather     55

ROBERT BURNS 1759–1796
   John Anderson my Jo     56
   Air     56

JOANNA BAILLIE 1762–1851
   A Child to his Sick Grandfather     58
   Hooly and Fairly     59

WILLIAM WORDSWORTH 1770–1850
   The Affliction of Margaret     61

SIR WALTER SCOTT 1771–1832
   Madge Wildfire Sings (from *The Heart of
   Midlothian*)     64

WALTER SAVAGE LANDOR 1775–1864
   The Maid's Lament     65

SIR HENRY TAYLOR 1800–1886
   Elena's Song     66

ELIZABETH BARRETT BROWNING 1806–1861
   A Man's Requirements     67

ALFRED, LORD TENNYSON 1809–1892
   Rizpah     69

WILLIAM BELL SCOTT 1811–1890
   The Witch's Ballad     73

ROBERT BROWNING 1812–1889
   A Woman's Last Word     78
   Any Wife to Any Husband     79

EMILY BRONTË 1818–1848
Song (The linnet in the rocky dells . . .)     84
CHRISTINA ROSSETTI 1830–1894
Amor Mundi     85
JOHN LEICESTER WARREN, LORD DE TABLEY
1835–1895
Nuptial Song (Sigh, heart, and break not . . .)     86
ALGERNON SWINBURNE 1837–1909
Anactoria     87
MARY E. TUCKER 1838?–?
Crazed     95
THOMAS HARDY 1840–1928
Circus-Rider to Ringmaster     96
ALICE MEYNELL 1847–1922
The Shepherdess     97
LOUISE IMOGEN GUINEY 1861–1920
The Wild Ride     98
The Knight Errant (Donatello's Saint George)     99
AMY LEVY 1861–1889
In the Mile End Road     100
RUDYARD KIPLING 1865–1936
Harp Song of the Dane Women     101
WILLIAM BUTLER YEATS 1865–1939
Crazy Jane On God     102
RICHARD LE GALLIENNE 1866–1947
Beauty Accurst     103
EDGAR LEE MASTERS 1869–1930
Jennie McGrew     105
Margaret Fuller Slack     106
CHARLOTTE MEW 1869–1928
The Farmer's Bride     107
ROBERT FROST 1874–1963
The Hill Wife     109
WALLACE STEVENS 1876–1955
The Plot Against the Giant     112
PRISCILLA JANE THOMPSON 1882–?
The Favorite Slave's Story     113
FANNIE STEARNS GIFFORD 1884–?
Moon Folly (from "The Songs of Conn the Fool")     119

# CONTENTS

EZRA POUND 1885–1972
The River Merchant's Wife: A Letter     121

H.D. 1886–1961
Hippolytus Temporizes     122

FENTON JOHNSON 1888–1958
The Scarlet Woman     124

CLAUDE MCKAY 1890–1948
The Wild Goat     125

EDNA ST. VINCENT MILLAY 1892–1950
Menses (He speaks, but to himself, being aware
how it is with her)     126

LOUISE BOGAN 1897–1970
The Crossed Apple     128

LANGSTON HUGHES 1902–1967
Madam and Her Madam     129

W.H. AUDEN 1907–1973
Miranda (excerpted from "The Sea and the Mirror")     130

THEODORE ROETHKE 1908–1963
Her Reticence     131

ELIZABETH BISHOP 1911–1979
Crusoe in England     132

MURIEL RUKEYSER 1913–1981
George Robinson: Blues     138

GWENDOLYN BROOKS 1917–
"Negro" Hero     140

MAY SWENSON 1919–1989
First Walk on the Moon     142

MONA VAN DUYN 1921–
The Gardener to His God     145

JOHN ASHBERY 1927–
On The Empress's Mind     146

ANNE SEXTON 1928–1974
Jesus Dies     147

RICHARD HOWARD 1929–
1915: A Pre-Raphaelite Ending, London     149

ADRIENNE RICH 1929–
The Loser     155

TED HUGHES 1930–
Cleopatra to the Asp     157

LUCILLE CLIFTON 1936–
powell (officer charged with the beating of rodney king)     158
ALICIA OSTRIKER 1937–
A Minor Van Gogh (He Speaks):     159
FRANK BIDART 1939–
Ellen West     160
SEAMUS HEANEY 1939–
Bog Queen     173
MICHAEL LONGLEY 1939–
Sulpicia     175
SUNITI NAMJOSHI 1941–
Caliban's Journal     176
MICHAEL HEFFERNAN 1942–
The Message     177
AI 1947–
The Good Shepherd: Atlanta, 1981     183
YUSEF KOMUNYAKAA 1947–
The Thorn Merchant's Mistress     185
HEATHER McHUGH 1948–
Note Delivered by Female Impersonator     187
DAVID ST. JOHN 1949–
Quote Me Wrong Again and I'll Slit the Throat of
Your Pet Iguana     188
RITA DOVE 1952–
Genie's Prayer Under the Kitchen Sink     190
ARCHIE WELLER 1957–
Ngungalari     192

The Cross-Gendered Poem     193
  *Dramatic monologue and the cross-gendered poem*     195
  *Rewriting Crusoe: subjectivity and agency in poetry*     199
  *Reading gender in cross-gendered verse*     200
  *Supplementing gender: other reading trajectories*     205
  *Some conclusions: understanding the place of cross-gendered verse*     209

Selected Bibliographies     211

# *Acknowledgements*

We wish to thank the following colleagues and readers for their help with the book: Robert Atwan, William Bartlett, Claire Beradini, Frank Bidart, Pete Caccavari, John Champagne, Susan Hahn, Daniel A. Harris, Michael Heffernan, Richard Howard, Cleoand George Kearns, Kristin Langellier, Lisa Merrill, Alicia Ostrica, Robert Richman, David St. John and William Wadsworth. In addition, we thank the Parsons School of Design for a faculty development grant which aided completion of the manuscript, as well as Thomas J. Reiter & Associates and the English Departments of Rutgers University and the University of St. Thomas for their support. Finally, thanks go to Talia Rodgers at Routledge for her invaluable advice and good humour.

The cover illustration, "Valentines" (1986) by Deborah Deichler, is used by permission of the artist and courtesy of Hollis Taggart Galleries, Inc., Washington D.C.

# *Permissions*

# *Introduction*

This project began in conversation. As a poet and literary critic, respectively, we have long been engaged in discussing the art and state of poetry; as teachers, these discussions have often led to consideration of available texts, and the sorts of collections which would be most useful in our classes. For years we talked. And over time it became clear that our conversations were less concerned with the vitality of poetry itself – which seems, as it always has, to be vital in some hands and less so in others – than with the ways readers might cultivate the new and the old together. What we wanted was an anthology that presented a wide historic and stylistic range of poems from a coherent perspective, a perspective that offered meaning to writers and readers alike.

We also had other goals in mind, goals born of our conversations. For instance, despite our generally different training as poet and critic, we found ourselves in surprising agreement over the interpretation of poetry: we both often endeavor to unlock a poem's meanings by way of its voice or "I." Moreover, while familiar with the conventional ways of addressing this subject – as a fiction, a mask, or even as the poet herself or himself – we had both come to the conclusion that these notions failed to account for every poem's construction, and particularly those contemporary poems which explore gender. Poetry had changed, and new poems were demanding a new way to be read. Part of our goal in compiling this anthology, then, came from the desire to address the "new" by examining changes in how poems use "I." Beginning with our conversations, and furthered by the making of a homemade anthology for a creative writing course, we began to uncover a wealth of poems that defy conventional opinions about voice. Most of these poems, as it turns out, are what we now call "cross-gendered verse."

The cross-gendered poem is one in which a woman writes in the voice of a man, or a man in the voice of a woman. A simple rhetorical move, but the more we thought about it, the more daring some of its implications seemed. In crossing gender as they create their personae, poets dramatize gender itself, bringing to the fore the ways in which a society standardizes social behavior – and often, in quite a few recent poems, challenge those standards. As we began to talk about this literary phenomenon, we soon realized that a great deal more of this poetry existed than we might have first thought. In fact, our anthology represents only a small percentage of poets who have written cross-gendered poems through the years. Each day we met in the hall, or later in the electronic hallway, would bring yet another example of poetry that met our simple criteria: a first-person monologue or lyric, sans exposition, which identifiably crossed gender. With each new conversation with colleagues, writers and readers alike, additional entries made their way onto our list – until, before we had set ourselves the task of compilation, the list exceeded the scope of a single volume.

Given the proliferation of the cross-gendered poem, we have endeavored to apply other, literary standards to the poems included here. From the start, we knew that we wanted a collection of *poetry* and not just a gimmick, poetry which was strong enough to engage readers and invite comment – poems that were literarily satisfying as well as representative of movements, positions and forms. The preponderance of the cross-gendered poem across periods and styles allowed us to meet this goal, and to exercise editorial choice without resorting to lesser works. As a result, the book's list of contents developed into our best argument for the importance of the cross-gendered poem.

This book presents the familiar alongside the new. Arranged chronologically by author's date of birth, these poems offer a wealth of ways to understand poetry, cross-gendered poetry and gender itself. Read consecutively, these poems also dramatize those ironies ever present in the study of literature – a few of which we have discussed in an essay at the end of the book, where we endeavor to consider the cross-gendered poem in relation to genre and theory, among other ideas. Here, then, we would like to record a few common characteristics of the poems, characteristics that offer the reader useful ways to begin thinking about cross-gendered verse.

Stylistically, these poems are as varied as any collection might be. From the complex monologues of Chaucer, Browning and Richard Howard to the declarative apostrophes of Edgar Lee Masters, Heather McHugh and Ai, the poems here make their meaning distinct and distinctly, especially as they often also cross race and sexuality. Thematic trends may be traced throughout, however, including avowals of revenge, betrayal and seduction; there are also "mad songs" and epistolary reversals, villanelles and blues. In short, the poems here provide literary evidence of human accomplishment, of rules and broken rules, form and radical innovation. What remains consistent through all this diversity, and proves a powerful lens, is the sense that each of these works should be seen within the context of gender and as an exploration of gender.

Feminist criticism has taught literary critics to read these acts of gender, while critical theories have allowed for new ways to work with text: but this is the first time the cross-gendered poem has been identified as a literary phenomenon. The reasons for this particular omission remain undocumented, although sexism itself has certainly contributed to the problem. Regardless, if prose has changed since Joyce's *Ulysses* (and, not incidentally, his Molly Bloom), then what might we say of poetry since Yeats' Crazy Jane or Bishop's Robinson Crusoe or Bidart's Ellen West – or whomever we elect to be poetry's radical cross-gendered icon? The works collected here prove worthy of such an argument: in its complexity, despite the demands of often mediocre conventions, the cross-gendered poem has thrived within and against the canon. What may be said of cross-gendered verse as a literary tradition remains uncharted; it is our hope that readers of this volume will welcome the opportunity to explore this terrain.

# *Poetry*

## GEOFFREY CHAUCER
### 1340?–1400

## *from The Prologe of the Wyves Tale of Bathe*

"Experience, though noon auctoritee
Were in this world, is right ynogh for me
To speke of wo that is in mariage;
For, lordynges, sith I twelve yeer was of age,
Thonked be God that is eterne on lyve,
Housbondes at chirche dore I have had fyve –
If I so ofte myghte have ywedded bee –
And all were worthy men in hir degree.
But me was toold, certeyn, nat longe agoon is,
That sith that Christ ne wente nevere but onis
To weddyng, in the Cane of Galilee,
That by the same ensample taughte he me
That I ne sholde wedded be but ones.
Herkne eek, lo, which a sharp word for the nones,
Biside a welle, Jhesus, God and man,
Spak in repreeve of the Samaritan:
"Thou hast yhad fyve housbondes," quod he,
"And that ilke man that now hath thee
Is noght thyn housbonde," thus seyde he certeyn.
What that he mente thereby, I kan nat seyn;
But that I axe, why that the fifthe man
Was noon housbonde to the Samaritan?
How manye myghte she have in mariage?
Yet herde I nevere tellen in my age
Upon this nombre diffinicioun.

Men may devyne and glosen, up and doun,
But wel I woot, expres, withoute lye,
God bad us for to wexe and multiplye;
That gentil text kan I wel understonde.
Eek wel I woot, he seyde myn housbonde
Sholde lete fader and mooder and take to me.
But of no nombre mencion made he,
Of bigamye, or of octogamye;
Why sholde men thanne speke of it vileynye?
  Lo, heere the wise king, daun Salomon;
I trowe he hadde wyves mo than oon.
As wolde God it leveful were unto me
To be refresshed half so ofte as he!
Which yifte of God hadde he for alle his wyvys!
No man hath swich that in this world alyve is.
God woot, this noble kyng, as to my wit,
The firste nyght had many a myrie fit
With ech of hem, so wel was hym on lyve.
Yblessed be God that I have wedded fyve!
[Of whiche I have pyked out the beste,
Bothe of here nether purs and of here cheste.
Diverse scoles maken parfyt clerkes,
And diverse practyk in many sondry werkes
Maketh the werkman parfyt sekirly;
Of fyve housbondes scoleiyng am I.]
Welcome the sixte, whan that evere he shal.
For sothe, I wol not kepe me chaast in al.
Whan myn housbonde is fro the world ygon,
Som Cristen man shal wedde me anon,
For thanne th'apostle seith that I am free
To wedde, a Goddes half, where it liketh me.
He seith that to be wedded is no synne;
Bet is to be wedded than to brynne.
What rekketh me, though folk seye vileynye
Of shrewed Lameth and his bigamye?
I woot wel Abraham was an hooly man,
And Jacob eek, as ferforth as I kan;
And ech of hem hadde wyves mo than two,
And many another holy man also.

Wher can ye seye, in any manere age,
That hye God defended mariage
By expres word? I pray yow, telleth me.
Or where commanded he virginitee?
I woot as wel as ye, it is no drede,
Th'apostel, whan he speketh of maydenhede,
He seyde that precept therof hadde he noon.
Men may conseille a womman to been oon,
But conseillyng is no commandement.
He putte it in oure owene juggement;
For hadde God comanded maydenhede,
Thanne hadde he dampned weddyng with the dede.
And certes, if ther were no seed ysowe,
Virginitee, thanne whereof sholde it growe?
Poul dorste nat comanden, atte leeste,
A thyng of which his maister yaf noon heeste.
The dart is set up for virginitee;
Cacche whoso may, who renneth best lat see.
    But this word is nat taken of every wight,
But ther as God lust gyve it of his myght.
I woot wel that th'apostel was a mayde;
But nathelees, though that he wroot and sayde
He wolde that every wight were swich as he,
Al nys but conseil to virginitee.
And for to been a wyf he yaf me leve
Of indulgence; so nys it no repreve
To wedde me, if that my make dye,
Withouten excepcion of bigamye.
Al were it good no womman for to touche –
He mente as in his bed or in his couche,
For peril is bothe fyr and tow t'assemble;
Ye knowe what this ensample may resemble.
This is al and som: he heeld virginitee
Moore parfit than weddyng in freletee
Freletee clepe I, but if that he and she
Wolde leden al hir lyf in chastitee.
    I graunte it wel; I have noon envie,
Though maydenhede preferre bigamye.
It liketh hem to be clene, body and goost;

Of my estaat I nyl nat make no boost,
For wel ye knowe, a lord in his houshold,
He nath nat every vessel al of gold;
Somme been of tree, and doon hir lord servyse.
God clepeth folk to him in sondry wyse,
And everich hath of God a propre yifte –
Som this, som that, as hym liketh shifte.
   Virginitee is greet perfeccion,
And continence eek with devocion,
But Crist, that of perfeccion is welle,
Bad nat every wight he shoulde go selle
Al that he hadde, and gyve it to the poore,
And in swich wise folwe hym and his foore.
He spak to hem that wolde lyve parfitly;
And lordynges, by youre leve, that am nat I.
I wol bistowe the flour of al myn age
In the acts and in fruyt of mariage.
   Telle me also, to what conclusion
Were membres maad of generacion,
And of so parfit wys a wright ywroght?
Trusteth right wel, they were nat maad for noght.
Glose whoso wole, and seye bothe up and doun
That they were maked for purgacioun
Of uryne, and our bothe thynges smale
Were eek to knowe a femele from a male,
And for noon oother cause – say ye no?
The experience woot wel it is noght so.
So that the clerkes be nat with me wrothe,
I sey this: that they maked ben for bothe;
That is to seye, for office and fore ese
Of engendrure, ther we nat God displese.
Why sholde men elles in hir bookes sette
That man shal yelde to his wyf hire dette?
Now wherwith sholde he make his paiement,
If he ne used his sely instrument?
Thanne were they maad upon a creature
To purge uryne, and eek for engendrure.
   But I seye noght that every wight is holde,
That hath swich harneys as I to yow tolde,

To goon and usen hem in engendrure.
Thanne sholde men take of chastitee no cure.
Crist was mayde and shapen as a man,
And many a seint, sith that the world bigan;
Yet lyved they evere in parfit chastitee.
I nyl envye no virginitee.
Lat hem be breed of pured whete-seed,
And lat us wyves hoten barly-breed;
And yet with barly-breed, Mark telle kan,
Oure Lord Jhesu refresshed many a man.
In swich estaat as God hath cleped us
I wol persevere; I nam nat precius.
In wyfhod I wol use myn instrument
As frely as my Makere hath it sent.
If I be daungerous, God yeve me sorwe!
Myn housbonde shal it have bothe eve and morwe,
Whan that hym list come forth and paye his dette.
An housbonde I wol have – I wol nat lette –
Which shal be bothe my dettour and my thral,
And have his tribulacion withal
Upon his flessh, whil that I am his wyf.
I have the power durynge al my lyf
Upon his propre body, and noght he.
Right thus the Apostel tolde it unto me,
And bad oure housbondes for to love us weel.
Al this sentence me liketh every deel" . . .

## GLOSSARY

*ben* be
*clepe* call
*eek* also
*engendrure* procreation
*everich* every
*ferforth* far
*freletee* weakness
*glosen* interpret
*heeste* commandment
*hoten* called
*ilke* very

*kan* know
*leden* lead
*lete* leave
*leveful* allowed
*nether purs* male genitals
*nys* is not
*on lyve* in life
*parfyt* perfect
*practyk* practice
*rekketh* care

*scoleiyng* schooling
*sekirly* certainly
*sely* innocent
*sorwe* sorrow
*thynges smale* genitals
*tow* flax
*wight* man
*woot* know
*wys* is
*yaf* gave
*yifte* gift

# WILLIAM DUNBAR
## 1460?–1520?

## *The Tua Mariit Wemen and the Wedo*

### *The Widow Has Buried*
### *Her Second Husband*

... "Deid is now that dyvour and dollin in erd:
With him deit all my dule and my dreary thoghtis;
Now done is my dolly nyght, my day is upsprungin;
Adew dolour, adew! my daynté now begynis!
Now am I a wedow iwise, and weill am at ese!
I weip as I wer woful, but wel is me for ever;
I busk as I wer bailfull, bot blith is my hert;
My mouth it makis murnyng, and my mynd lauchis;
My clokis thai ar caerfull in colour of sabill,
Bot courtly and ryght curyus my corse is therundir:
I drup with a ded luke in my dulé habit,
As with manis daill I had done for dayis of my lif.
   "Quhen that I go to the kirk, cled in cair-weid,
As foxe in lambis fleise fenye I my cheir;
Than lay I furght my bright buke on breid on my kne,
With mony lusty lettir ellummynit with gold;
And drawis my clok forthwart our my face quhit,
That I may spy unaspyit a space me beside:
Full oft I blenk by my buke, and blynis of devotion,
To se quhat berne is best brand or bredest in schulderis,
Or forgeit is maist forcely to furnyse a bancat
In Venus chalmer valyeandly withoutin vane ruse.
And as the new mone all pale oppressit with change,
Kythis quhilis her cleir face through cluddis of sable,
So keik I through my clokis, and castis kynd lukis
To knychtis, and to cleirkis, and cortly personis.
   Quhen frendis of my husbandis behaldis me on fer,
I haif a wattir spunge for wa, within my wyde clokis,
Than wring I it full wylély and wetis my chekis;

With that wattiris myn ene and weltiris doune teris.
Than way thai all that sittis about "Se ye nought, allace!
Yone lustlese led, so lelely scho luffit hir husband;
Yone is a peté to enprent in a princis hert,
That sic a perle of plesance suld yone pane dre!"
I sane me as I war ane sanct, and semys ane angell;
At langage of lichory I leit as I war crabit:
I sich, without sair her or seiknes in body;
According to my sable weid I mon haif sad maneris,
Or thai will se all the suth; for certis we wemen
We set ws all fra the syght to syle men of treuth:
We dule for na evill dead, so it be derne haldin.
     "Wise wemen has wayis and wondirfull gydingis
With gret engyne to bejaip ther jolyus husbandis
And quyetly with sic craft convoyis our materis
That under Crist no creatur kennis of our doingis.
Bot folk a cury may miscuke that knawledge wantis,
And has na colouris for to cover thair awne kindly fautis;
As dois thir damysellis for derne dotit lufe
That dogonis haldis in dainté and delis with thaim so lang,
Quhill all the cuntré knaw ther kyndnes and faith:
Faith has a fair name, bot falsheid faris bettir:
Fy on hir that can nought feyne her fame for to saif!
Yit am I wise in sic werk and wes all my tyme;
Thoght I want wit in warldlynes I wylis haif in luf,
As ony happy woman has that is of hie blude:
Hutit be the halok lase a hundir yeir of eild!
I have ane secrete serwand, rycht sobir of his toung,
That me supportis of sic nedis quhen I a syne mak:
Thoght he be sympill to the sicht, he has a tong sicker;
Full mony semelyar sege wer service dois mak
Thoght I haif cair undir cloke the cleir day quhill nyght,
Yit haif I solace undir serk quhill the sone ryse.
Yit am I haldin a haly wif our all the haill schyre:
I am sa peteouse to the pur quhen ther is personis mony;
In passing of pilgrymage I pride me full mekle,
Mair for the prese of peple na ony perdoun wynyng.
     "Bot yit me think the best bourd, quhen baronis and knychtis
And othir bachilleris, blith blwmyng in youth,

And all my luffaris lele my lugeng persewis
And fyllis me wyne wantonly with weilfair and joy:
Sum rownis, and sum ralyeis; and sum redis ballatis;
Sum raiffis furght rudly with riatus speche;
Sum plenis, and sum prayis; sum prasis mi bewté;
Sum kissis me; sum clappis me; sum kyndnes me proferis;
Sum kerffis to me curtasli; sum me the cop giffis;
Sum stalwardly steppis ben with a stout curage
And a stif standand thing staiffis in my neiff;
And mony blenkis ben our, that but full fer sittis,
That mai for the thik thrang nought thrif as thai wald.
Bot, with my fair calling I comfort thaim all:
For he that sittis me nixt, I nip on his finger;
I serf him on the tothir syde on the samin fasson;
And he that behind me sittis, I hard on him lene;
And him befor, with my fut fast on his I stramp;
And to the bernis far but sueit blenkis I cast;
To every man in speciall speke I sum wordis
So wisly and so womanly quhill warmys ther hertis.
That is no liffand laid so law of degré
That sall me luf unluffit, I am so loik-hertit;
And gif his lust so be lent into my lyre quhit
That he be lost or with me lig, his lif sall not danger.
I am so mercifull in mynd, and menys all wichtis,
My sely saull sal be saif, quhen Sabot all jugis.
Ladyis, leir thir lessonis and be no lassis fundin:
This is the legeand of my lif, thought Latyne it be nane."
   Quhan endit had her ornat speche this eloquent wedow,
Lowd thai lewch all the laif, and loffit hir mekle,
And said thai suld exampill tak of her soverane teching
And wirk efter her wordis, that woman wes so prudent.
Than culit thai thair mouthis with confortable drinkis
And carpit full cummerlik with cop going round . . .

## Translation by Mark Willhardt

... "Dead is now that blackguard and buried in earth;
With him died my dull and dreary thoughts;
Now done is my dispirited night, my day is sprung up;
Adieu, dolor, adieu! My delight now begins!
Now am I a wise widow, and am well at ease!
I weep as I were woeful, but I am well forever;
I dress as I were distressed, but delighted is my heart;
My mouth it makes mourning, but my mind laughs;
My clothes they are careful in color of sable,
But beautiful and sumptuous my body is under all:
I droop with a dead look in my dull habit,
As for man's part I had done for days of my life.
   "When I go to the church, clad in mourning clothes,
As a fox in lamb's fleece I find my chair;
Then I lay first my bright book broad on my knee,
With many lusty letters illumined with gold;
And draw my cloak forward over my face white,
So I may spy unspied a space beside me;
Full oft I wink from my book and, blind to devotion,
See what man is the best flame or has the broadest shoulders,
Nor overlook which most fiercely could furnish a banquet
In Venus' chamber valiantly and without vain lies.
And as the new moon all pale oppressed with change,
Makes meanwhile her clear face through clouds of sable,
So peep I though my clothes, and cast kind looks
To knights, and to clerks, and courtly persons.
   "When friends of my husband's behold me from afar,
I have a water sponge for them, within my wide robes,
Then I wring it full subtlely and wet my cheeks;
With that, my eyes water and welter down tears.
Then they all say that sit about, "See you nought, alas!
One listlessly laid, so truly she loved her husband;
Yon is a pity to imprint on a prince's heart,
That such a pearl of pleasure should have a troubled head!"
I behave as I were a saint, and seem an angel;
At lecherous language I start as if angry:
I am such, without sore heart or sickness in body;

According to my sable weeds I must have sad manners,
Or they will see all the truth; for certainly we women
We set us all from the sight to deceive men of truth:
We sorrow for no evil deed, so it be held in secret.
   "Wise women have ways and wonderful maneuvers
With great devices to fool their happy husbands
And coyly with such craft convey our matters
That under Christ no creature knows of our doings –
But folk a curry may miscook who knowledge want,
And have no color for to cover their own kindly faults;
As do their damsels for secret irrational love
That men hold in delight and deal with them so long,
While all the country know their kindness and faith:
Faith has a fair name, but falsehood fares better:
Fie on her that cannot fan her passion for to save it!
Yet am I wise in such work and was all my time;
Though I want wit in worldliness, I have wiles in love,
As any happy woman has that is of high blood:
Reviled be the giddy girl turned a hundred years old!
I have a secret servant, right sober of his tongue,
That supports me of such needs when I make a sign:
Though he be simple to the sight, he has a certain tongue;
Full many similar sages wary service do make
Though I have care under my cloak the clear day while night,
Yet have I solace under my surplice while the sun rises.
Yet am I remaining a holy wife over all the whole shire;
I am so piteous to the poor when there are many people;
In passing of pilgrimage I pride myself full greatly,
More for the praise of people than any pardon winning.
   "But yet I think the best sport, when barons and knights
And other bachelors, blithe in blooming youth,
And all my loyal lovers pursuing my lodging
And fill my wine wantonly with welfare and joy:
Some roam and so speak vehemently; and some read ballads;
Some roughs fight rudely with riotous speech;
Some play and some pray; some praise my beauty;
Some kiss me; some smack me; some offer me kindness;
Some bow to me courteously; some give me the cup;
Some stalwartly step up with stout courage

And a stiff standing thing stuff in my hand;
And many winks be ours, that wait full far away,
That may for the thick throng nought thrive as they would.
But, with my fair calling I comfort them all:
For he that sits next to me, I nip on his finger;
I serve him on the other side in the same fashion;
And he that sits behind me, I hard on him lean;
And him before, with my foot fast on his I stroke;
And to the men far but sweet winks I cast;
To every man in special I speak some words,
So wisely and so womanly, which warm their hearts.
There is no lover laid so low of degree
That shall me leave unloved, I am so like-hearted;
And if his lust so be lent into my lyre white
That he be lost or lie with me, his life shall not danger.
I am so merciful in mind, and men all muscular and valiant,
My true soul shall be safe, when Sunday judges all.
Ladies, learn these lessons and be no lass taken advantage of:
This is the lesson of my life, though Latin it be none."
   When ended had her ornate speech this eloquent widow,
Loud they laughed all the day and loved her greatly,
And said they should take example of her sovereign teaching
And work after her words, that woman was so prudent.
Then cooled they their mouths with comforting drinks
And gabbed full friendly with the cup going round . . .

# NICHOLAS BRETON
## 1545?–1626?

## *A Sweet Lullaby*

Come, little babe; come, silly soul,
Thy father's shame, thy mother's grief,
Born, as I doubt, to all our dole
And to thyself unhappy chief:
   Sing lullaby, and lap it warm,
   Poor soul that thinks no creature harm.

Thou little think'st and less dost know
The cause of this thy mother's moan,
Thou want'st the wit to wail her woe,
And I myself am all alone.
   Why dost thou weep? why dost thou wail?
   And knowest not yet what thou dost ail.

Come, little wretch – ah, silly heart,
Mine only joy, what can I more?
If there be any wrong thy smart,
That may the destinies implore,
   'Twas I, I say, against my will;
   I wail the time, but be thou still.

And dost thou smile? Oh, thy sweet face,
Would God himself he might thee see;
No doubt thou wouldst soon purchase grace,
I know right well, for thee and me.
   But come to mother, babe, and play,
   For father false is fled away.

Sweet boy, if it by fortune chance
Thy father home again to send,
If death do strike me with his lance,
Yet mayst thou me to him commend;
   If any ask thy mother's name,
   Tell how by love she purchased blame.

Then will his gentle heart soon yield;
I know him of a noble mind.
Although a lion in the field,
A lamb in town thou shalt him find.
    Ask blessing, babe, be not afraid;
    His sugared words hath me betrayed.

Then mayst thou joy and be right glad,
Although in woe I seem to moan.
Thy father is no rascal lad,
A noble youth of blood and bone;
    His glancing looks, if he once smile,
    Right honest women may beguile.

Come, little boy, and rock asleep,
Sing lullaby, and be thou still;
I that can do nought else but weep
Will sit by thee and wail my fill.
    God bless my babe, and lullaby,
    From this thy father's quality.

## SIR WALTER RALEIGH
### 1552?–1618

# *The Nymph's Reply to the Shepherd*

If all the world and love were young,
And truth in every shepherd's tongue,
These pretty pleasures might me move
To live with thee and be thy love.

Time drives the flocks from field to fold,
When rivers rage and rocks grow cold;
And Philomel becometh dumb;
The rest complains of cares to come.

The flowers do fade, and wanton fields
To wayward winter reckoning yields:
A honey tongue, a heart of gall,
Is fancy's spring, but sorrow's fall.

Thy gowns, thy shoes, thy bed of roses,
Thy cap, thy kirtle, and thy posies
Soon break, soon wither, soon forgotten,
In folly ripe, in reason rotten.

Thy belt of straw and ivy buds,
Thy coral clasps and amber studs,
All these in me no means can move
To come to thee and be thy love.

But could youth last, and love still breed,
Had joys no date, nor age no need,
Then these delights my mind might move
To live with thee and be thy love.

# THOMAS LODGE
## 1558?–1625

## *Rosalind's Madrigal*

Love in my bosom like a bee
    Doth suck his sweet;
Now with his wings he plays with me,
    Now with his feet.
Within mine eyes he makes his nest,
His bed amidst my tender breast,
My kisses are his daily feast,
And yet he robs me of my rest –
    Ah, wanton, will ye?

And if I sleep, then percheth he
    With pretty flight,
And makes his pillow of my knee
    The livelong night.
Strike I my lute, he tunes the string,
He music plays if so I sing,
He lends me every lovely thing,
Yet cruel he my heart doth sting –
    Whist, wanton, still ye!

Else I with roses every day
    Will whip you hence,
And bind you, when you long to play,
    For your offence.
I'll shut mine eyes to keep you in,
I'll make you fast it for your sin,
I'll count your power not worth a pin;
Alas! what hereby shall I win
    If he gainsay me?

What if I beat the wanton boy
    With many a rod?
He will repay me with annoy,
    Because a god.

Then sit thou safely on my knee,
And let thy bower my bosom be,
Lurk in mine eyes, I like of thee.
O Cupid, so thou pity me,
　　Spare not, but play thee!

# ROBERT GREENE
## 1560–1592

## *The Shepherd's Wife's Song*

Ah, what is love? It is a pretty thing,
As sweet unto a shepherd as a king –
   And sweeter too,
For kings have cares that wait upon a crown,
And cares can make the sweetest love to frown.
   Ah then, ah then,
If country loves such sweet desires do gain,
What lady would not love a shepherd swain?

His flocks once folded, he comes home at night
As merry as a king in his delight –
   And merrier too,
For kings bethink them what the state require,
Where shepherds careless carol by the fire.
   Ah then, ah then,
If country loves such sweet desires gain,
What lady would not love a shepherd swain?

He kisseth first, then sits as blithe to eat
His cream and curds as doth the king his meat –
   And blither too,
For kings have often fears when they do sup,
Where shepherds dread no poison in their cup.
   Ah then, ah then,
If country loves such sweet desires gain,
What lady would not love a shepherd swain?

To bed he goes, as wanton then, I ween,
As is a king in dalliance with a queen –
   More wanton too,
For kings have many griefs, affects to move,
Where shepherds have no greater grief than love.
   Ah then, ah then,
If country loves such sweet desires gain,
What lady would not love a shepherd swain?

Upon his couch of straw he sleeps as sound
As doth the king upon his beds of down –
    More sounder too,
For cares cause kings full oft their sleep to spill,
Where weary shepherds lie and snort their fill.
    Ah then, ah then,
If country loves such sweet desires gain,
What lady would not love a shepherd swain?

Thus with his wife he spends the year, as blithe
As doth the king, at every tide or sithe –
    And blither too,
For kings have wars and broils to take in hand,
Where shepherds laugh and love upon the land.
    Ah then, ah then,
If country loves such sweet desires gain,
What lady would not love a shepherd swain?

# JOHN DONNE
## 1572–1631

## *Sapho To Philaenis*

Where is that holy fire, which Verse is said
   To have, is that inchanting force decai'd?
Verse that drawes Natures workes, from Natures law,
   Thee, her best worke, to her worke cannot draw.
Have my teares quench'd my old Poetique fire;
   Why quench'd they not as well, that of desire?
Thoughts, my mindes creatures, often are with thee,
   But I, their maker, want their libertie.
Onely thine image, in my heart, doth sit,
   But that is waxe, and fires environ it.
My fires have driven, thine have drawne it hence;
   And I am rob'd of Picture, Heart, and Sense.
Dwells with me still mine irksome Memory,
   Which, both to keepe, and lose, grieves equally.
That tells me'how faire thou art: Thou art so faire,
   As, gods, when gods to thee I doe compare,
Are grac'd thereby; And to make blinde men see,
   What things gods are, I say they'are like to thee.
For, if we justly call each silly man
   A litle world, What shall we call thee than?
Thou art not soft, and cleare, and strait, and faire,
   As Down, as Stars, Cedars, and Lillies are,
But thy right hand, and cheek, and eye, only
   Are like thy other hand, and cheek, and eye.
Such was my *Phao* awhile, but shall be never,
   As thou, wast, art, and, oh, maist thou be ever.
Here lovers sweare in their Idolatrie,
   That I am such; but Griefe discolors me.
And yet I grieve the lesse, least Griefe remove
   My beauty,'and make me'unworthy of thy love.
Plaies some soft boy with thee, oh there wants yet
   A mutuall feeling which should sweeten it.
His chinne, a thorny hairy'unevennesse

Doth threaten, and some daily change possesse.
Thy body is a naturall Paradise,
   In whose selfe, unmanur'd, all pleasure lies,
Nor needs perfection; why shouldst thou than
   Admit the tillage of a harsh rough man?
Men leave behinde them that which their sin showes,
   And are as theeves trac'd, which rob when it snowes.
But of our dallyance no more signes there are,
   Then fishes leave in streames, or Birds in aire.
And betweene us all sweetnesse may be had;
   All, all that Nature yields, or Art can adde.
My two lips, eyes, thighs, differ from thy two,
   But so, as thine from one another doe;
And, oh, no more; the likenesse being such,
   Why should they not alike in all parts touch?
Hand to strange hand, lippe to lippe none denies;
   Why should they brest to brest, or thighs to thighs?
Likenesse begets such strange selfe flatterie,
   That touching my selfe, all seemes done to thee.
My selfe I'embrace, and mine owne hands I kisse,
   And amorously thanke my selfe for this.
Me, in my glasse, I call thee; But, alas,
   When I would kisse, teares dimme mine eyes, and glasse.
O cure this loving madnesse, and restore
   Me to mee; thee, my halfe, my all, my more.
So may thy cheekes red outweare scarlet dye,
   And their white, whitenesse of the Galaxy,
So may thy mighty,'amazing beauty move
   Envy'in all women, and in all men, love,
And so be change, and sicknesse, farre from thee,
   As thou by comming neere, keep'st them from me.

## MARY SIDNEY WROTH,
## COUNTESS OF MONTGOMERY
### 1586?–1640?

# *The Duke's Song*

If a clear fountain still keeping a sad course
  Weep out her sorrows in drops, which like tears fall,
  Marvel not if I lament my misfortune,
    brought to the same call.

Who thought such fair eyes could shine, and dissemble?
  Who thought such sweet breath could poison love's shame?
  Who thought those chaste ears could so be defiled?
    hers be the sole blame.

While love deserved love, of mine still she failed not,
  Fool I to love still where mine was neglected,
  Yet faith and honor, both of me claimed it,
    although rejected.

Oft have I heard her vow, never sweet quiet
  Could once possess her while that I was else where,
  But words were breath then, and as breath they wasted
    into a lost air.

So soon is love lost, not in heart imprinted,
  Silly I, knew not the false power of changing,
  Love I expected, yet, ah, was deceived,
    more her fond ranging.

Infant Love tied me not to mistrust change,
  Vows kept me fearless, yet all those were broken:
  Love, faith, and friendship by her are dissolved,
    suffered unspoken.

# ROBERT HERRICK
## 1591–1674

## *The Mad Maid's Song*

Good morrow to the day so fair;
  Good morning, sir, to you;
Good morrow to mine own torn hair,
  Bedabbled with the dew.

Good morning to this primrose too;
  Good morrow to each maid,
That will with flowers the tomb bestrew
  Wherein my love is laid.

Ah woe is me, woe, woe is me,
  Alack and welladay!
For pity, sir, find out that bee,
  Which bore my love away.

I'll seek him in your bonnet brave;
  I'll seek him in your eyes;
Nay, now I think they've made his grave
  I' the bed of strawberries.

I'll seek him there; I know, ere this,
  The cold, cold earth doth shake him;
But I will go, or send a kiss
  By you, sir, to awake him.

Pray hurt him not; though he be dead,
  He knows well who do love him,
And who with green turfs rear his head,
  And who do rudely move him.

He's soft and tender; pray take heed;
  With bands of cowslips bind him,
And bring him home; – but 'tis decreed
  That I shall never find him.

# ANDREW MARVELL
## 1621–1678

## *The Nymph Complaining For the Death of Her Fawn*

The wanton troopers riding by
Have shot my fawn, and it will die.
Ungentle men! They cannot thrive
To kill thee. Thou ne'er didst alive
Them any harm, alas, nor could
Thy death yet do them any good.
I'm sure I never wished them ill,
Nor do I for all this, nor will;
But if my simple prayers may yet
Prevail with heaven to forget
Thy murder, I will join my tears
Rather than fail. But oh, my fears!
It cannot die so. Heaven's King
Keeps register of everything,
And nothing may we use in vain.
Ev'n beasts must be with justice slain,
Else men are made their deodands;
Though they should wash their guilty hands,
In this warm life-blood, which doth part
From thine, and wound me to the heart,
Yet could they not be clean, their stain
Is dyed in such a purple grain.
There is not such another in
The world to offer for their sin.
　　Unconstant Sylvio, when yet
I had not found him counterfeit,
One morning (I remember well)
Tied in this silver chain and bell,
Gave it to me: nay, and I know
What he said then; I'm sure I do:
Said he: "Look how your huntsman here

Hath taught a fawn to hunt his dear."
But Sylvio soon had me beguiled;
This waxèd tame, while he grew wild,
And quite regardless of my smart,
Left me his fawn, but took his heart.

    Thenceforth, I set myself to play
My solitary time away
With this, and very well content,
Could so mine idle life have spent;
For it was full of sport and light
Of foot and heart, and did invite
Me to its game: it seemed to bless
Itself in me; how could I less
Than love it? Oh, I cannot be
Unkind to a beast that loveth me.

    Had it lived long, I do not know
Whether it too might have done so
As Sylvio did; his gifts might be
Perhaps as false, or more, than he;
But I am sure, for aught that I
Could in so short a time espy,
Thy love was far more better than
The love of false and cruel men.

    With sweetest milk and sugar, first
I it at mine own fingers nursed;
And as it grew, so every day
It waxed more white and sweet than they.
It had so sweet a breath! And oft
I blushed to see its foot more soft
And white, shall I say than my hand?
Nay, any lady's of the land.

    It is a wondrous thing how fleet
'Twas on those little silver feet;
With what a pretty skipping grace
It oft would challenge me the race;
And when it had left me far away,
'Twould stay, and run again, and stay;
For it was nimbler much than hinds,
And trod as if on the four winds.

I have a garden of my own,
But so with roses overgrown,
And lilies, that you would it guess
To be a little wilderness;
And all the springtime of the year
It only lovèd to be there.
Among the beds of lilies I
Have sought it oft, where it should lie,
Yet could not, till itself would rise,
Find it, although before mine eyes;
For, in the flaxen lilies' shade,
It like a bank of lilies laid.
Upon the roses it would feed,
Until its lips e'en seemed to bleed;
And then to me 'twould boldly trip,
And print those roses on my lip.
But all its chief delight was still
On roses thus itself to fill,
And its pure virgin limbs to fold
In whitest sheets of lilies cold:
Had it lived long, it would have been
Lilies without, roses within.
  O help! O help! I see it faint
And die as calmly as a saint!
See how it weeps! the tears do come
Sad, slowly dropping like a gum.
So weeps the wounded balsam; so
The holy frankincense doth flow;
The brotherless Heliades
Melt in such amber tears as these.
  I in a golden vial will
Keep these two crystal tears, and fill
It till it do o'erflow with mine;
Then place it in Diana's shrine.
  Now my sweet fawn is vanished to
Whither the swans and turtles go,
In fair Elysium to endure,
With milk-white lambs and ermines pure.
O do not run too fast; for I

Will but bespeak thy grave, and die.
  First, my unhappy statue shall
Be cut in marble, and withal
Let it be weeping, too; but there
Th' engraver sure his art may spare;
For I so truly thee bemoan
That I shall weep, though I be stone,
Until my tears, still dropping, wear
My breast, themselves engraving there.
There at my feet shalt thou be laid,
Of purest alabaster made;
For I would have thine image be
White as I can, though not as thee.

# JOHN DRYDEN
## 1631–1700

## *Farewell, Ungrateful Traitor*

Farewell, ungrateful traitor,
   Farewell, my perjured swain,
Let never injured creature
   Believe a man again.
The pleasure of possessing
Surpasses all expressing,
But 'tis too short ablessing,
   And love too long a pain.

'Tis easy to deceive us
   In pity of your pain,
But when we love, you leave us
   To rail at you in vain.
Before we have descried it,
There is no bliss beside it,
But she that once has tried it,
   Will never love again.

The passion you pretended
   Was only to obtain;
But when the charm is ended
   The charmer you disdain.
Your love by ours we measure,
Till we have lost our treasure,
But dying is a pleasure,
   When loving is a pain.

## APHRA BEHN
### 1640–1689

## *The Dream*
### *(from "A Voyage to the Isle of Love")*

All trembling in my arms Aminta lay,
Defending of the bliss I strove to take;
Raising my rapture by her kind delay,
Her force so charming was and weak.
The soft resistance did betray the grant,
While I pressed on the heaven of my desires;
Her rising breasts with nimbler motions pant;
Her dying eyes assume new fires.
Now to the height of languishment she grows,
And still her looks new charms put on;
– Now the last mystery of Love she knows,
We sigh, and kiss: I waked, and all was done.

'Twas but a dream, yet by my heart I knew,
Which still was panting, part of it was true:
Oh how I strove the rest to have believed;
Ashamed and angry to be undeceived!

## *Silvio's Complaint:*
## *A Song, To a Fine Scotch Tune*

### I
In the Blooming Time o'th'year,
In the Royal Month of *May:*
Au the Heaves were glad and clear,
Au the Earth was Fresh and Gay.
A Noble Youth but all Forlorn,
Lig'd Sighing by a Spring:
'Twere better I's was nere Born,
    Ere wisht to be a King.

## II

Then from his Starry Eyne,
Muckle Showers of Christal Fell:
To bedew the Roses Fine,
That on his Cheeks did dwell.
And ever 'twixt his Sighs he'd cry,
How Bonny a Lad I'd been,
Had I, weys me, nere Aim'd high,
   Or wisht to be a King.

## III

With Dying Clowdy Looks,
Au the Filed sof Groves he kens:
Au the Gleeding Murmuring Brooks,
(Noo his Unambitious Friends)
Toe which he eance with Mickle Cheer
His Bleating Flocks woud bring:
And crys, woud God I'd dy'd here,
   Ere wisht to be a King.

## IV

How oft in Yonder Mead,
Cover'd orc with Painted Flowers:
Au the Dancing Youth I've led,
Where we past our Blether Hours.
In Yonder Shade, in Yonder Grove,
How Blest the *Nymphs* have been:
Ere I for Pow'r Debaucht Love,
   Or wisht to be a King.

## V

Not au the *Arcadian Swains*,
In their Pride and Glory Clad:
Not au the Spacious Plains,
Ere Coud Boast a Bleether Lad.
When ere I Pip'd, or Danc'd, or Ran,
Or leapt, or whirl'd the Sling:
The Flowry Wreaths I still won,
   And wisht to be a King.

## VI

But Curst be yon Tall Oak,
And Old *Thirsis* be accurst:
There I first my peace forsook,
There I learnt Ambition first.
Such glorious Songs of *Hero's* Crown'd,
The Restless Swain woud Sing:
My Sould unknown desires found,
  And Languisht to be King.

## VII

Ye Garlands wither now,
Fickle Glories vanish all:
Ye Wreaths that deckt my Brow,
To the ground neglected fall.
No more my sweet Repose molest,
Nor to my Fancies bring
The Golden Dreams of being Blest
  With Titles of a King.

## VIII

Ye Noble Youths beware,
Shun Ambitious powerful Tales:
Distructive, False, and Fair,
Like the Oceans Flattering Gales.
See how my Youth and Glories lye,
Like Blasted Flowers i'th' Spring:
My Fame Renown and all dye,
  For wishing to be King.

# ALEXANDER POPE
## 1688–1744

## *Eloisa to Abelard*

### The Argument

Abelard *and* Eloisa *flourish'd in the twelfth Century; they were two of the most distinguish'd persons of their age in learning and beauty, but for nothing more famous than for their unfortunate passion. After a long course of Calamities, they retired each to a several Convent, and consecrated the remainder of their days to religion. It was many years after this separation, that a letter of* Abelard's *to a Friend which contain'd the history of his misfortunes, fell into the hands of* Eloisa. *This awakening all her tenderness, occasion'd those celebrated letters (out of which the following is partly extracted) which give so lively a picture of the struggles of grace and nature, virtue and passion.*

IN these deep solitudes and awful cells,
Where heav'nly-pensive, contemplation dwells,
And ever-musing melancholoy reigns;
What means this tumult in a Vestal's veins?
Why rove my thoughts beyond this last retreat?
Why feels my heart its long-forgotten heat?
Yet, yet I love! – From *Abelard* it came,
And *Eloisa* yet must kiss the name.
    Dear fatal name! rest ever unreveal'd.
Nor pass these lips in holy silence seal'd.
Hide it, my heart, within that close disguise,
Where, mix'd with God's, his lov'd Idea lies.
Oh write it not, my hand – The name appears
Already written – wash it out, my tears!
In vain lost *Eloisa* weeps and prays,
Her heart still dictates, and her hand obeys.
    Relentless walls! whose darksom round contains
Repentant sighs, and voluntary pains:
Ye rugged rocks! which holy knees have worn;
Ye grots and caverns shagg'd with horrid thorn!

Shrines! where their vigils pale-ey'd virgins keep,
And pitying saints, whose statues learn to weep!
Tho' cold like you, unmov'd, and silent grown,
I have not yet forgot my self to stone.
All is not Heav'n's while *Abelard* has part,
Still rebel nature holds out half my heart;
Nor pray'rs nor fasts its stubborn pulse restrain,
Nor tears, for ages, taught to flow in vain.
    Soon as thy letter trembling I unclose,
That well-known name awakens all my woes.
Oh name for ever sad! for ever dear!
Still breath'd in sighs, still usher'd with a tear.
I tremble too where-e'er my own I find,
Some dire misfortune follows close behind.
Line after line my gushing eyes o'erflow,
Led thro' a sad variety of woe:
Now warm in love, now with'ring in thy bloom,
Lost in a convent's solitary gloom!
There stern religion quench'd th' unwilling flame,
There dy'd the best of passions, Love and Fame.
    Yet write, oh write me all, that I may join
Griefs to thy griefs, and eccho sighs to thine.
Nor foes nor fortune take this pow'r away.
And is my *Abelard* less kind than they?
Tears are still mine, and those I need not spare,
Love but demands what else were shed in pray'r;
No happier task these faded eyes pursue,
To read and weep is all they now can do.
    Then share thy pain, allow that sad relief;
Ah more than share it! give me all thy grief.
Heav'n first taught letters for some wretches aid,
Some banish'd lover, or some captive maid;
They live, they speak, they breathe what love inspires,
Warm from the soul, and faithful to its fires,
The virgin's wish without her fears impart,
Excuse the blush, and pour out all the heart,
Speed the soft intercourse from soul to soul,
And waft a sigh from *Indus* to the *Pole*.
    Thou know'st how guiltless first I met thy flame,

When Love approach'd me under Friendship's name;
My fancy form'd thee of Angelick kind,
Some emanation of th' all-beauteous Mind.
Those smiling eyes, attemp'ring ev'ry ray,
Shone sweetly lambent with celestial day:
Guiltless I gaz'd; heav'n listen'd while you sung;
And truths divine came mended from that tongue.
From lips like those what precept fail'd to move?
Too soon they taught me 'twas no sin to love.
Back thro' the paths of pleasing sense I ran,
Nor wish'd an Angel whom I lov'd a Man.
Dim and remote the joys of saints I see,
Nor envy them, that heav'n I lose for thee.
   How oft', when press'd to marriage, I have said,
Curse on all laws but those which love has made!
Love, free as air, at sight of human ties,
Spread his light wings, and in a moment flies.
Let wealth, let honour, wait the wedded dame,
August her deed, and sacred be her fame;
Before true passion all those views remove,
Fame, wealth, and honour! what are you to Love?
The jealous God, when we profane his fires,
Those restless passions in revenge inspires;
And bids them make mistaken mortals groan,
And seek in love for ought but love alone.
Should at my feet the world's great master fall,
Himself, his throne, his world, I'd scorn 'em all:
Not *Caesar's* empress wou'd I deign to prove;
No, make me mistress to the man I love;
If there be yet another name more free,
More fond than mistress, make me that to thee!
Oh happy state! when souls each other draw,
When love is liberty, and nature, law:
All then is full, possessing, and possest,
No craving Void left aking in the breast:
Ev'n thought meets thought e'er from the lips it part,
And each warm wish springs mutual from the heart.
This sure is bliss (if bliss on earth there be)
And once the lot of *Abelard* and me.

Alas how chang'd! what sudden horrors rise!
A naked Lover bound and bleeding lies!
Where, where was *Eloise*? her voice, her hand,
Her ponyard, had oppos'd the dire comand.
Barbarian stay! that bloody stroke restrain;
The crime was common, common be the pain.
I can no more; by shame, by rage supprest,
Let tears, and burning blushes speak the rest.
   Canst thou forget that sad, that solemn day,
When victims at yon' altar's foot we lay?
Canst thou forget what tears that moment fell,
When, warm in youth, I bade the world farewell?
As with cold lips I kiss'd the sacred veil,
The shrines all trembled, and the lamps grew pale:
Heav'n scarce believ'd the conquest it survey'd,
And Saints with wonder heard the vows I made.
Yet then, to those dread altars as I drew,
Not on the Cross my eyes were fix'd, but you;
Not grace, or zeal, love only was my call,
And if I lose thy love, I lose my all.
Come! with thy looks, thy words, relieve my woe;
Those still at least are left thee to bestow.
Still on that breast enamour'd let me lie,
Still drink delicious poison from thy eye,
Pant on thy lip, and to thy heart be prest;
Give all thou canst – and let me dream the rest.
Ah no! instruct me other joys to prize,
With other beauties charm my partial eyes,
Full in my view set all the bright abode,
And make my soul quit *Abelard* for God.
   Ah think at least thy flock deserves thy care,
Plants of thy hand, and children of thy pray'r.
From the false world in early youth they fled,
By thee to mountains, wilds, and deserts led.
You rais'd these hallow'd walls; the desert smil'd,
And Paradise was open'd in the Wild.
No weeping orphan saw his father's stores
Our shrines irradiate, or emblaze the floors;
No silver saints, by dying misers giv'n,

Here brib'd the rage of ill-requited heav'n:
But such plain roofs as piety could raise,
And only vocal with the Maker's praise.
In these lone walls (their day's eternal bound)
These moss-grown domes with spiry turrets crown'd,
Where awful arches make a noon-day night,
And the dim windows shed a solemn light;
Thy eyes diffus'd a reconciling ray,
And gleams of glory brighten'd all the day.
But now no face divine contentment wears,
'Tis all blank sadness, or continual tears.
See how the force of others' pray'rs I try,
(Oh pious fraud of am'rous charity!)
But why should I on others' pray'rs depend?
Come thou, my father, brother, husband, friend!
Ah let thy handmaid, sister, daughter move,
And, all those tender names in one, thy love!
The darksom pines that o'er yon' rocks reclin'd
Wave high, and murmur to the hollow wind,
The wandring streams that shine between the hills,
The grots that eccho to the trinklings rills,
The dying gales that pant upon the trees,
The lakes that quiver to the curling breeze;
No more these scenes my meditation aid,
Or lull to rest the visionary maid:
But o'er the twilight groves, and dusky caves,
Long-sounding isles, and intermingled graves,
Black Melancholy sits, and round her throws
A death-like silence, and dread repose:
Her gloomy presence saddens all the scene,
Shades ev'ry flow'r, and darkens ev'ry green,
Deepens the murmur of the falling floods,
And breathes a browner horror on the woods.
   Yet here for ever, ever must I stay;
Sad proof how well a lover can obey!
Death, only death, can break the lasting chain;
And here ev'n then, shall my cold dust remain,
Here all its frailties, all its flames resign,
And wait, till 'tis no sin to mix with thine.

Ah wretch! believ'd the spouse of God in vain,
Confess'd within the slave of love and man.
Assist me heav'n! but whence arose that pray'r?
Sprung it from piety, or from despair?
Ev'n here, where frozen chastity retires,
Love finds an altar for forbidden fires.
I ought to grieve, but cannot what I ought;
I mourn the lover, not lament the fault;
I view my crime, but kindle at the view,
Repent old pleasures, and sollicit new:
Now turn'd to heav'n, I weep my past offence,
Now think of thee, and curse my innocence.
Of all affliction taught a lover yet,
'Tis sure the hardest science to forget!
How shall I lose the sin, yet keep the sense,
And love th' offender, yet detest th' offence?
How the dear object from the crime remove,
Or how distinguish penitance from love?
Unequal task! a passion to resign,
For hearts so touch'd, so pierc'd, so lost as mine.
E'er such a soul regains its peaceful state,
How often must it love, how often hate!
How often, hope, despair, resent, regret,
Conceal, disdain – do all things but forget.
But let heav'n seize it, all at once 'tis fir'd,
Not touch'd, but rapt; not waken'd, but inspir'd!
Oh come! oh teach me nature to subdue,
Renounce my love, my life, my self – and you.
Fill my fond heart with God alone, for he
Alone can rival, and succeed to thee.
   How happy is the blameless Vestal's lot!
The world forgetting, by the world forgot.
Eternal sun-shine of the spotless mind!
Each pray'r accepted, and each wish resign'd;
Labour and rest, that equal periods keep;
"Obedient slumbers that can wake and weep";
Desires compos'd, affection ever ev'n,
Tears that delight, and sighs that waft to heav'n.
Grace shines around her with serenest beams,

And whisp'ring Angels prompt her golden dreams.
For her th' unfading rose of *Eden* blooms,
And wings of Seraphs shed divine perfumes;
For her the Spouse prepares the bridal ring,
For her white virgins *Hymenoeals* sing;
To sounds of heav'nly harps, she dies away,
And melts in visions of eternal day.
   Far other dreams my erring soul employ,
Far other raptures, of unholy joy:
When at the close of each sad, sorrowing day,
Fancy restores what vengeance snatch'd away,
Then conscience sleeps, and leaving nature free,
All my loose soul unbounded springs to thee.
O curst, dear horrors of all-conscious night!
How glowing guilt exalts the keen delight!
Provoking Dæmons all restraint remove,
And stir within me ev'ry source of love.
I hear thee, view thee, gaze o'er all thy charms,
And round thy phantom glue my clasping arms.
I wake – no more I hear, no more I view,
The phantom flies me, as unkind as you.
I call aloud; it hears not what I say;
I stretch my empty arms; it glides away;
To dream once more I close my willing eyes;
Ye soft illusions, dear deceits, arise!
Alas no more! – methinks we wandring go
Thro' dreary wastes, and weep each other's woe;
Where round some mould'ring tow'r pale ivy creeps,
And low-brow'd rocks hang nodding o'er the deeps.
Sudden you mount! you beckon from the skies;
Clouds interpose, waves roar, and winds arise.
I shriek, start up, the same sad prospect find,
And wake to all the griefs I left behind.
   For thee the fates, severely kind, ordain
A cool suspense from pleasure and from pain;
Thy life a long, dead calm of fix'd repose;
No pulse that riots, and no blood that glows.
Still as the sea, e'er winds were taught to blow,
Or moving spirit bade the waters flow;

Soft as the slumbers of a saint forgiv'n,
And mild as opening gleams of promis'd heav'n.
   Come *Abelard*! for what has thou to dread?
The torch of *Venus* burns not for the dead;
Nature stands check'd; Religion disapproves;
Ev'n thou art cold – yet *Eloisa* loves.
Ah hopeless, lasting flames! like those that burn
To light the dead, and warm th' unfruitful urn.
   What scenes appear where-e'er I turn my view!
The dear Ideas, where I fly, pursue,
Rise in the grove, before the altar rise,
Stain all my soul, and wanton in my eyes!
I waste the Matin lamp in sighs for thee,
Thy image steals between my God and me,
Thy voice I seem in ev'ry hymn to hear;
With ev'ry bead I drop too soft a tear.
When from the Censer clouds of fragrance roll,
And swelling organs lift the rising soul;
One thought of thee puts all the pomp to flight,
Priests, Tapers, Temples, swim before my sight:
In seas of flame my plunging soul is drown'd,
While Altars blaze, and Angels tremble round.
   While prostrate here in humble grief I lie,
Kind, virtuous drops just gath'ring in my eye,
While praying, trembling, in the dusts I roll,
And dawning grace is opening on my soul:
Come, if thou dar'st, all charming as thou art!
Oppose thy self to heav'n; dispute my heart;
Come, with one glance of those deluding eyes,
Blot out each bright Idea of the skies.
Take back that grace, those sorrows, and those tears,
Take back my fruitless penitence and pray'rs,
Snatch me, just mounting, from the blest abode,
Assist the Fiends and tear me from my God!
   No, fly me, fly me! far as Pole from Pole;
Rise *Alps* between us! and whole oceans roll!
Ah come not, write not, think not once of me,
Nor share one pang of all I felt for thee.
Thy oaths I quit, thy memory resign,

Forget, renounce me, hate whate'er was mine.
Fair eyes, and tempting looks (which yet I view!)
Long lov'd, ador'd ideas! all adieu!
O grace serene! oh virtue heav'nly fair!
Divine oblivion of low-thoughted care!
Fresh blooming hope, gay daughter of the sky!
And faith, our early immortality!
Enter each mild, each amicable guest;
Receive, and wrap me in eternal rest!
   See in her Cell sad *Eloisa* spread,
Propt on some tomb, a neighbour of the dead!
In each low wind methinks a Spirit calls,
And more than Echoes talk along the walls.
Here, as I watch'd the dying lamps around,
From yonder shrine I heard a hollow sound.
Come, sister come! (it said, or seem'd to say)
Thy place is here, sad sister come away!
Once like thy self, I trembled, wept, and pray'd,
Love's victim then, tho' now a sainted maid:
But all is calm in this eternal sleep;
Here grief forgets to groan, and love to weep,
Ev'n superstition loses ev'ry fear:
For God, not man, absolves our frailties here.
   I come, I come! prepare your roseate bow'rs,
Celestial palms, and ever blooming flowr's.
Thither, where sinners may have rest, I go,
Where flames refin'd in breast seraphic glow.
Thou, *Abelard*! the last sad office pay,
And smooth my passage to the realms of day:
See my lips tremble, and my eye-balls roll,
Suck my last breath, and catch my flying soul!
Ah no – in sacred vestments may'st thou stand,
The hallow'd taper trembling in thy hand,
Present the Cross before my lifted eye,
Teach me at once, and learn of me to die.
Ah then, thy once-lov'd *Eloisa* see!
It will be then no crime to gaze on me.
See from my cheek the transient roses fly!
See the last sparkle languish in my eye!

Till ev'ry motion, pulse, and breath, be o'er;
And ev'n my *Abelard* be lov'd no more.
O death all-eloquent! you only prove
What dust we doat on, when 'tis man we love.
   Then too, when fate shall thy fair frame destroy,
(That cause of all my guilt, and all my joy)
In trance extatic may thy pangs be drown'd,
Bright clouds descend, and Angels watch thee round,
From opening skies may streaming glories shine,
And Saints embrace thee with a love like mine.
   May one kind grave unite each hapless name,
And graft my love immortal on thy fame.
Then, ages hence, when all my woes are o'er,
When this rebellious heart shall beat no more;
If ever chance two wandring lovers brings
To *Paraclete's* white walls, and silver springs,
O'er the pale marble shall they join their heads,
And drink the falling tears each other sheds,
Then sadly say, with mutual pity mov'd,
Oh may we never love as these have lov'd!
From the full quire when loud *Hosanna's* rise,
And swell the pomp of dreadful sacrifice,
Amid that scene, if some relenting eye
Glance on that stone where our cold reliques lie,
Devotion's self shall steal a thought from heav'n,
One human tear shall drop, and be forgiv'n.
And sure if fate some future Bard shall join
In sad similitude of griefs to mine,
Condemn'd whole years in absence to deplore,
And image charms he must behold no more,
Such if there be, who loves so long, so well;
Let him our sad, our tender story tell;
The well-sung woes will sooth my pensive ghost;
He best can paint 'em, who shall feel 'em most.

# MARY MONCK
## 1690?–1715

## *On A Romantic Lady*

This poring over your *Grand Cyrus*
Must ruin you and will quite tire us.
It makes you think that an affront 'tis,
Unless your lover's an Orontes,
And courts you with a passion frantic,
In manner and in style romantic.
Now though I count myself no zero,
I don't pretend to be an hero,
Or a by-blow of him that thunders,
Nor are you one of the Sev'n Wonders,
But a young damsel very pretty,
And your true name is Mistress Betty.

# JUDITH MADAN
## 1702–1781

## *Abelard to Eloisa*

In my dark cell, low prostrate on the ground,
Mourning my crimes, thy letter entrance found;
Too soon my soul the well-known name confest,
My beating heart sprung fiercely in my breast,
Thro' my whole frame a guilty transport glow'd,
And streaming torrents from my eyes fast flow'd.
  O *Eloisa*! art thou still the same?
Dost thou still nourish this destructive flame?
Have not the gentle rules of peace and heav'n
From thy soft soul this fatal passion driv'n?
Alas! I thought you disengag'd and free;
And can you still, still sigh and weep for me?
What powerful deity, what hallow'd shrine,
Can save me from a love, a faith like thine?
Where shall I fly, when not this awful cave
Whose rugged feet the surging billows lave,
When not those gloomy cloister solemn walls,
O'er whose rough sides the languid ivy crawls,
When my dread vows, in vain, their force oppose?
Oppos'd to love – alas! – how vain are vows?
In fruitless penitence I wear away,
Each tedious night, and sad revolving day;
I fast, I pray, and with deceitful art,
Veil thy dear image in my tortur'd heart;
My tortur'd heart conflicting passions move,
I hope, despair, repent – yet still I love:
A thousand jarring thoughts my bosom tear,
For thou, not God, O Eloise, art there.
To the false world's deluding pleasures dead,
Nor longer by its wand'ring fires misled,
In learn'd disputes harsh precepts I infuse,
And give the counsel I want pow'r to use.
The rigid maxims of the brave and wise

[46]

Have quench'd each milder sparkle of my eyes;
Each lovely feature of this once lov'd face,
By grief revers'd, assumes a sterner grace:
O Eloisa! should the fates once more,
Indulgent to my view, thy charms restore,
How from my arms would'st thou with horror start
To miss the form familiar to thy heart!
Nought could thy quick, thy piercing judgment see
To speak me *Abelard* – but love to thee.
Lean abstinence, pale grief, and haggard care,
The dire attendants of forlorn despair,
Have *Abelard* the young, the gay, remov'd,
And in the hermit sunk the man you lov'd.
Wrapt in the gloom of these holy mansions shed,
The thorny paths of penitence I tread;
Lost to the world, from all its interests free,
And torn from all my soul held dear in thee,
Ambition with its trail of frailties gone,
All loves and forms forgot – but thine alone,
Amid the blaze of day, the dusk of night,
My *Eloisa* rises to my sight;
Veil'd as in *Paraclet's* secluded tow'rs
The wretched mourner counts the lagging hours,
I hear her sighs, see the swift falling tears,
Weep all her griefs, and pant with all her cares.
O vows! O convent! your stern force impart,
And frown the melting phantom from my heart;
Let other sighs a worthier sorrow show,
Let other tears from sin repentant flow:
Low to the earth my guilty eyes I roll,
And humble to the dust my heaving soul.
Forgiving pow'r! thy gracious call I meet,
Who first impower'd this rebel heart to beat;
Who through this trembling, this offending frame,
For nobler ends inspir'd life's active flame.
O! change the temper of this lab'ring breast,
And form anew each beating pulse to rest!
Let springing grace, fair faith, and hope remove
The fatal traces of destructive love!

Destructive love from his warm mansions tear,
And leave no tracks of *Eloisa* there!
   Are these the wishes of my inmost soul?
Would I its soft, its tend'rest sense control?
Would I this touch'd, this glowing heart refine
To the cold substance of this marble shrine?
Transform'd like these pale swarms that round me move,
Of blest insensibles – who know no love?
Ah! rather let me keep this hapless flame,
Adieu! false honour, unavailing fame!
Nor your harsh rules, but tender love supplies
The streams that gush from my despairing eyes;
I feel the traitor melt about my heart,
And thro' my veins with treach'rous influence dart;
Inspire me, heav'n! assist me, grace divine!
Aid me, ye saints! unknown to pains like mine;
You! who on earth serene all griefs could prove,
All but the tort'ring pangs of hopeless love;
A holier rage in your pure bosoms dwelt,
Nor can you pity what you never felt:
A sympathizing grief alone can lure,
The hand that heals must feel what I endure.
Thou, *Eloise*, alone canst give me ease,
And bid my struggling soul subside to peace;
Restore me to my long-lost heav'n of rest,
And take thyself from my reluctant breast;
If crimes like mine could an allay receive,
That blest allay thy wond'rous charms might give.
   Thy form that first to love my heart inclin'd,
Still wanders in my lost, my guilty mind.
I saw thee as the new-blown blossoms fair,
Sprightly as light, more soft than summer's air,
Bright as their beams thy eyes a mind disclose,
Whilst on thy lips gay blush'd the fragrant rose;
Wit, youth, and love, in each dear feature shone,
Prest by my fate, I gaz'd – and was undone.
   There dy'd the gen'rous fire, whose vig'rous flame
Enlarg'd my soul, and urg'd me on to fame.
Nor fame, nor wealth, my soften'd heart could move,

Dully insensible to all but love.
Snatch'd from myself, my learning tasteless grew,
Vain my philosophy oppos'd to you;
A train of woes succeed, nor should we mourn
The hours that cannot, ought not to return.

As once to love I sway'd your yielding mind
To find, alas! too fatally inclin'd,
To virtue now let me your breast inspire,
And fan, with zeal divine, the heav'nly fire;
Teach you to injur'd heav'n all chang'd to turn,
And bid the soul with sacred rapture burn.
O! that my own example might impart
This noble warmth to your soft trembling heart!
That mine with pious undissembled care
Could aid the latent virtue struggling there.

Alas! I rave – nor grace, nor zeal divine
Burn in a heart oppress'd with crimes like mine.
Too sure I find, while I the tortures prove
Of feeble piety, conflicting love,
On black despair my forc'd devotions built;
Absence for me has sharper pangs than guilt.
Yet, yet, my *Eloise*, thy charms I view,
Yet my sighs breathe, my tears pour forth for you;
Each weak resistance stronger knits my chain,
I sigh, weep, love, despair, repent – in vain.
Haste, *Eloisa*, haste, your lover free,
Amidst your warmest pray'r – O, think on me!
Wing with your rising zeal my grov'ling mind,
And let me mine from your repentance find!
Ah! labour, strive, your love, yourself control!
The change will sure affect my kindred soul;
In blest content our purer sighs shall breathe,
And heav'n assisting, shall our crimes forgive.
But if unhappy, wretched, lost, in vain,
Faintly th'unequal combat you sustain;
If not to heav'n you feel your bosom rise,
Nor tears refin'd fall contrite from your eyes;
If still your heart its wanted passions move,
If still, to speak all pains in one – you love;

Deaf to the weak essays of living breath,
Attend the stronger eloquence of death.
When that kind pow'r this captive soul shall free,
Which only then can cease to doat on thee;
When gently sunk to my eternal sleep,
The *Paraclete* my peaceful urn shall keep;
Then, *Eloisa*, then your lover view,
See his quench'd eyes no longer gaze on you;
From their dead orbs that tender utt'rance flown,
Which first to thine my heart's soft fate made known.
This breast no more, at length to ease consign'd,
Pant like the waving aspen in the wind;
See all my wild, tumultuous passion o'er,
And thou, amazing change! belov'd no more;
Behold the destin'd end of human love –
But let the sight your zeal alone improve;
Let not your conscious soul, to sorrow mov'd,
Recall how much, how tenderly I lov'd:
With pious care your fruitless griefs restrain,
Nor let a tear your sacred veil profane:
Nor e'en a sigh on my cold urn bestow,
But let your breast with new-born raptures glow;
Let love divine frail mortal love dethrone
And to your mind immortal joys make known;
Let heav'n relenting strike your ravish'd view,
And still the bright, the blest pursuit renew!
So with your crimes shall your misfortune cease,
And your rack'd soul be calmly hush'd to peace.

# MARY LEAPOR
## 1722–1746

## *Strephon to Celia.*
## *A Modern Love-Letter*

MADAM,
       I hope you'll think it's true
I deeply am in love with you,
When I assure you t'other day,
As I was musing on my way,
At thought of you I tumbled down
Directly in a deadly swoon:
And though 'tis true I'm something better,
Yet I can hardly spell my letter:
And as the latter you may view,
I hope you'll think the former true.
You need not wonder at my flame,
For you are not a mortal dame:
I saw you dropping from the skies;
And let dull idiots swear your eyes
With love their glowing breast inspire,
I tell you they are flames of fire,
That scorch my forehead to a cinder,
And burn my very heart to tinder.
Your breast so mighty cold, I trow,
Is made of nothing else but snow:
Your hands (no wonder they have charms)
Are made of ivory like your arms.
Your cheeks, that look as if they bled,
Are nothing else but roses red.
Your lips are coral very bright,
Your teeth – though numbers out of spite
May say they're bones – yet 'twill appear
They're rows of pearl exceeding dear.

Now, madam, as the chat goes round,
I hear you have ten thousand pound:
But that as I a trifle hold,
Give me your person, dem your gold;
Yet for your own sake 'tis secured,
I hope – your houses too insured;
I'd have you take a special care,
And of false mortgages beware;
You've wealth enough 'tis true, but yet
You want a friend to manage it.
Now such a friend you soon might have,
By fixing on your humble slave;
Not that I mind a stately house,
Or value money of a louse;
But your five hundred pounds a year,
I would secure it for my dear:
Then smile upon your slave, that lies
Half murdered by your radiant eyes;
Or else this very moment dies –
STREPHON

# WILLIAM BLAKE
## 1757–1827

## *Nurse's Song*

When the voices of children are heard on the green,
And laughing is heard on the hill,
My heart is at rest within my breast,
And everything else is still.

"Then come home, my children, the sun is gone down
And the dews of night arise;
Come, come, leave off play, and let us away
Till the morning appears in the skies."

"No, no, let us play, for it is yet day,
And we cannot go to sleep;
Besides, in the sky the little birds fly,
And the hills are all covered with sheep."

"Well, well, go and play till the light fades away,
And then go home to bed."
The little ones leaped and shouted and laughed,
And all the hills echoed.

## *The Angel*

I dreamt a dream – what can it mean?
And that I was a maiden queen,
Guarded by an angel mild –
Witless woe was ne'er beguiled!

And I wept both night and day,
And he wiped my tears away,
And I wept both day and night
And hid from him my heart's delight.

So he took his wings and fled.
Then the morn blushed rosy red;

I dried my tears and armed my fears
With ten thousand shields and spears.

Soon my angel came again;
I was armed, he came in vain.
For the time of youth was fled,
And grey hairs were on my head.

## Song
### (My silks and fine array . . .)

My silks and fine array,
  My smiles and languish'd air,
By love are driv'n away;
  And mournful lean Despair
Brings me yew to deck my grave:
Such end true lovers have.

His face is fair as heav'n,
  When springing buds unfold;
O why to him was't giv'n,
  Whose heart is wintry cold?
His breast is love's all worship'd tomb,
Where all love's pilgrims come.

Bring me an axe and spade,
  Bring me a winding sheet;
When I my grave have made,
  Let winds and tempests beat:
Then down I'll lie, as cold as clay.
True love doth pass away!

## JEAN GLOVER
### 1758–1801

# *O'er the Muir Amang the Heather*

Coming through the Craigs o' Kyle,
  Amang the bonnie blooming heather,
There I met a bonnie lassie,
  Keeping a' her ewes thegither.

  O'er the muir amang the heather,
  O'er the muir amang the heather,
  There I met a bonnie lassie,
  Keeping a' her ewes thegither.

Says I, "My dear, where is thy hame?
  In muir or dale, pray tell me whether?"
Says she, "I tent the fleecy flocks
  That feed amang the blooming heather."

We laid us down upon a bank,
  Sae warm and sunny was the weather;
She left her flocks at large to rove
  Amang the bonnie blooming heather.

While thus we lay she sung a sang,
  Til echo rang a male and farther;
And aye the burden o' the sang
  Was "O'er the muir amang the heather."

She charmed my heart, and aye sinsyne
  I couldna think on ony ither:
By sea and sky she shall be mine,
  The bonnie lass amang the heather!

  O'er the muir amang the heather,
  Down amang the blooming heather: –
  By sea and sky she shall be mine,
  The bonnie lass amang the heather!

# ROBERT BURNS
## 1759–1796

## *John Anderson my Jo*

John Anderson, my jo, John,
  When we were first acquent,
Your locks were like the raven,
  Your bonnie brow was brent;
But now your brow is beld, John,
  Your locks are like the snow;
But blessings on your frosty pow,
  John Anderson, my jo.

John Anderson, my jo, John,
  We clamb the hill thegither;
And mony a cantie day, John,
  We've had wi' ane anither:
Now we maun totter down, John,
  And hand in hand we'll go,
And sleep thegither at the foot,
  John Anderson, my jo.

## *Air*

I once was a maid, though I cannot tell when,
And still my delight is in proper young men:
Some one of a troop of dragoons was my daddie,
No wonder I'm fond of a sodger laddie.
  Sing lal de dal &c.

The first of my loves was a swaggering blade,
To rattle the thundering drum was his trade;
His leg was so tight and his cheek was so ruddy,
Transported I was with my sodger laddie.

But the godly old chaplain left him in the lurch,
The sword I forsook for the sake of the church;

He ventured the soul, and I risked the body,
'Twas then I proved false to my sodger laddie.

Full soon I grew sick of my sanctified sot,
The regiment at large for a husband I got;
From the gilded spontoon to the fife I was ready;
I asked no more but a sodger laddie.

But the peace it reduced me to beg in despair,
Till I met my old boy in a Cunningham fair;
His rags regimental they fluttered so gaudy,
My heart it rejoiced at a sodger laddie.

And now I have lived – I know not how long,
And still I can join in a cup and a song;
But whilst with both hands I can hold the glass steady,
Here's to thee, my hero, my sodger laddie.

# JOANNA BAILLIE
## 1762–1851

# *A Child to his Sick Grandfather*

Grand-Dad, they say you're old and frail,
Your stockèd legs begin to fail:
Your knobbèd stick (that was my horse)
Can scarce support your bended corse;
While back to wall you lean so sad,
   I'm vexed to see you, dad.

You used to smile and stroke my head,
And tell me how good children did;
But now, I wot not how it be,
You take me seldom on your knee;
Yet ne'ertheless I am right glad
   To sit beside you, dad.

How lank and thin your beard hangs down!
Scant are the white hairs on your crown;
How wan and hollow are your cheeks!
Your brow is rough with crossing breaks;
But yet, for all his strength is fled,
   I love my own old dad.

The housewives round their potions brew,
And gossips come to ask for you:
And for your weal each neighbour cares,
And good men kneel, and say their pray'rs:
And ev'rybody looks so sad,
   When you are ailing, dad.

You will not die, and leave us then?
Rouse up and be our dad again.
When you are quiet and laid in bed,
We'll doff our shoes and softly tread:
And when you wake we'll aye be near,
   To fill old dad his cheer.

When through the house you shift your stand,
I'll lead you kindly by the hand;
When dinner's set, I'll with you bide,
And aye be serving by your side;
And when the weary fire burns blue,
   I'll sit and talk with you.

I have a tale both long and good,
About a partlet and her brood;
And cunning greedy fox that stole,
By dead of midnight, through a hole,
Which slyly to the hen-roost led –
   You love a story, dad?

And then I have a wond'rous tale
Of men all clad in coats of mail,
With glitt'ring swords – you nod, I think?
Your fixèd eyes begin to wink;
Down your bosom sinks your head;
   You do not hear me, dad.

## Hooly and Fairly

### (Founded on an old Scotch song)

Oh, neighbours! what had I a-do for to marry!
My wife she drinks posset and wine o' Canary,
And ca's me a niggardly, thraw-gabbit cairly,
   O, gin my wife wad drink hooly and fairly!
   Hooly and fairly, hooly and fairly,
   O, gin my wife wad drink hooly and fairly!

She sups wi' her kimmers on dainties enow,
Aye bowing and smirking and wiping her mou',
While I sit aside, and am helpit but sparely,
   O, gin my wife wad feast hooly and fairly!
   Hooly and fairly, hooly and fairly,
   O, gin my wife wad feast hooly and fairly!

To fairs and to bridals and preachings and a',
She gangs sae light headed and buskit sae braw,
In ribbons and mantuas that gar me gae barely!
   O, gin my wife wad spend hooly and fairly!
   Hooly and fairly, hooly and fairly,
   O, gin my wife wad spend hooly and fairly!

I' the kirk sic commotion last Sabbath she made,
Wi' babs o' red roses and breast-knots o'erlaid!
The Dominie stickit the psalm very nearly:
   O, gin my wife wad dress hooly and fairly!
   Hooly and fairly, hooly and fairly,
   O, gin my wife wad dress hooly and fairly!

She's warring and flyting frae morning till e'en,
And if ye gainsay her, her een glow'r sae keen,
Then tongue, nieve, and cudgel she'll lay on ye sairly:
   O, gin my wife wad strike hooly and fairly!
   Hooly and fairly, hooly and fairly,
   O, gin my wife wad strike hooly and fairly!

When tired wi' her cantrips, she lies in her bed,
The wark a' negleckit, the chaumer unred,
While a' our guid neighbours are stirring so early:
   O, gin my wife wad wurk timely and fairly!
   Timely and fairly, timely and fairly,
   O, gin my wife wad wurk timely and fairly!

A word o' guid counsel or grace she'll hear none;
She bandies the Elders, and mocks at Mess John,
While back in his teeth his own text she flings rarely:
   O, gin my wife wad speak hooly and fairly!
   Hooly and fairly, hooly and fairly,
   O, gin my wife wad speak hooly and fairly!

I wish I were single, I wish I were freed;
I wish I were doited, I wish I were dead,
Or she in the mouls, to dement me nae mair, lay!
   What does it 'vail to cry hooly and fairly,
   Hooly and fairly, hooly and fairly,
   Wasting my breath to cry hooly and fairly!

# WILLIAM WORDSWORTH
## 1770–1850

## *The Affliction of Margaret*

Where art thou, my beloved Son,
Where art thou, worse to me than dead?
Oh find me, prosperous or undone!
Or, if the grave be now thy bed,
Why am I ignorant of the same
That I may rest; and neither blame,
Nor sorrow may attend thy name?

Seven years, alas, to have received
No tidings of an only child;
To have despair'd, and have believ'd,
And be for evermore beguil'd;
Sometimes with thoughts of very bliss!
I catch at them, and then I miss;
Was ever darkness like to this?

He was among the prime in worth,
An object beauteous to behold;
Well born, well bred; I sent him forth
Ingenuous, innocent, and bold:
If things ensued that wanted grace,
As hath been said, they were not base;
And never blush was on my face.

Ah! little doth the Young One dream,
When full of play and childish cares,
What power hath even his wildest scream,
Heard by his Mother unawares!
He knows it not, he cannot guess:
Years to a Mother bring distress;
But do not make her love the less.

Neglect me! no I suffer'd long
From that ill thought; and being blind,
Said, "Pride shall help me in my wrong;

[61]

Kind mother have I been, as kind
As ever breathed:" and that is true;
I've wet my path with tears like dew,
Weeping for him when no one knew.

My Son, if thou be humbled, poor,
Hopeless of honour and of gain,
Oh! do not dread thy mother's door;
Think not of me with grief and pain:
I now can see with better eyes;
And worldly grandeur I despise,
And fortune with her gifts and lies.

Alas! the fowls of Heaven have wings,
And blasts of Heaven will aid their flight;
They mount, how short a voyage brings
The Wanderers back to their delight!
Chains tie us down by land and sea;
And wishes, vain as mine, may be
All that is left to comfort thee.

Perhaps some dungeon hears thee groan,
Maim'd, mangled by inhuman men;
Or thou upon a Desart thrown
Inheritest the Lion's Den;
Or hast been summoned to the Deep,
Thou, Thou and all thy mates, to keep
An incommunicable sleep.

I look for Ghosts; but none will force
Their way to me; 'tis falsely said
That there was ever intercourse
Betwixt the living and the dead;
For, surely, then I should have sight
Of Him I wait for day and night,
With love and longings infinite.

My apprehensions come in crowds;
I dread the rustling of the grass;
The very shadows of the clouds
Have power to shake me as they pass:

I question things, and do not find
One that will answer to my mind;
And all the world appears unkind.

Beyond participation lie
My troubles, and beyond relief:
If any chance to heave a sigh
They pity me, and not my grief.
Then come to me, my Son, or send
Some tidings that my woes may end;
I have no other earthly friend.

# SIR WALTER SCOTT
## 1771–1832

## *Madge Wildfire Sings*
### *(from The Heart of Midlothian)*

Proud Maisie is in the wood,
  Walking so early;
Sweet Robin sits on the bush,
  Singing so rarely.

"Tell me, thou bonny bird,
  When shall I marry me?" –
"When six braw gentlemen
  Kirkward shall carry ye."

"Who makes the bridal bed,
  Birdie, say truly?"
"The grey-headed sexton
  That delves the grave duly."

"The glow-worm o'er grave and stone
  Shall light thee steady.
The owl from the steeple sing,
  'Welcome, proud lady.'"

# WALTER SAVAGE LANDOR
## 1775–1864

## *The Maid's Lament*

I loved him not; and yet, now he is gone,
   I feel I am alone.
I check'd him while he spoke; yet, could he speak,
   Alas! I would not check.
For reasons not to love him once I sought,
   And wearied all my thought
To vex myself and him: I now would give
   My love could he but live
Who lately lived for me, and, when he found
   'Twas vain, in holy ground
He hid his face amid the shades of death!
   I waste for him my breath
Who wasted his for me! but mine returns,
   And this lorn bosom burns
With stifling heat, heaving it up in sleep,
   And waking me to weep
Tears that had melted his soft heart: for years
   Wept he as bitter tears!
*Merciful God!* such was his latest prayer,
   *These may she never share!*
Quieter is his breath, his breast more cold,
   Than daisies in the mould,
Where children spell, athwart the churchyard gate,
   His name and life's brief date.
Pray for him, gentle souls, whoe'er you be,
   And, oh! pray too for me!

# SIR HENRY TAYLOR
## 1800–1886

## *Elena's Song*

Quoth tongue of neither maid nor wife
  To heart of neither wife nor maid,
Lead we not here a jolly life
  Betwixt the shine and shade?

Quoth heart of neither maid nor wife
  To tongue of neither wife nor maid,
Thou wag'st but I am worn with strife,
  And feel like flowers that fade.

# ELIZABETH BARRETT BROWNING
## 1806–1861

## *A Man's Requirements*

### I

Love me, sweet, with all thou art,
　Feeling, thinking, seeing, –
Love me in the lightest part,
　Love me in full being.

### II

Love me with thine open youth
　In its frank surrender;
With the vowing of thy mouth,
　With its silence tender.

### III

Love me with thine azure eyes,
　Made for earnest granting!
Taking color from the skies,
　Can Heaven's truth be wanting?

### IV

Love me with their lids, that fall
　Snow-like at first meeting:
Love me with thine heart, that all
　The neighbours then see beating.

### V

Love me with thine hand stretched out
　Freely – open-minded:
Love me with thy loitering foot, –
　Hearing one behind it.

### VI

Love me with thy voice, that turns
　Sudden faint above me;
Love me with thy blush that burns
　When I murmur "Love me!"

## VII

Love me with thy thinking soul –
  Break it to love-sighing;
Love me with thy thoughts that roll
  On through living – dying.

## VIII

Love me in thy gorgeous airs,
  When the world has crowned thee!
Love me, kneeling at thy prayers,
  With the angels round thee.

## IX

Love me pure, as musers do,
  Up the woodlands shady:
Love me gaily, fast, and true,
  As a winsome lady.

## X

Through all hopes that keep us brave,
  Further off or nigher,
Love me for the house and grave, –
  And for something higher.

## XI

Thus, if thou wilt prove me, dear,
  Woman's love no fable,
*I* will love *thee* – half-a-year –
  As a man is able.

# ALFRED, LORD TENNYSON
## 1809–1892

## *Rizpah*

### I

Wailing, wailing, wailing, the wind over the land and sea –
And Willy's voice in the wind, "O mother, come out to me."
Why should he call me tonight, when he knows that I cannot go?
For the downs are as bright as day, and the full moon stares at the
    snow.

### II

We should be seen, my dear; they would spy us out of the town.
The loud black nights for us, and the storm rushing over the down,
When I cannot see my own hand, but am led by the creak of the
    chain,
And grovel and grope for my son till I find myself drenched with
    the rain.

### III

Anything fallen again? nay – what was there left to fall?
I have taken them home, I have numbered the bones, I have hidden
    them all.
What am I saying? and what are *you*? do you come as a spy?
Falls? what falls? who knows? As the tree falls so must it lie.

### IV

Who let her in? how long has she been? you – what have you
    heard?
Why did you sit so quiet? you never have spoken a word.
O – to pray with me – yes – a lady – none of their spies –
But the night has crept into my heart, and begun to darken my
    eyes.

### V

Ah – you, that have lived so soft, what should *you* know of the
    night,
The blast and the burning shame and the bitter frost and the
    fright?

[69]

I have done it, while you were asleep – you were only made for the
　day.
I have gathered my baby together – and now you may go your way.

## VI

Nay – for it's kind of you, Madam, to sit by an old dying wife.
But say nothing hard of my boy, I have only an hour of life.
I kissed my boy in the prison, before he went out to die.
"They dared me to do it," he said, and he never has told me a lie.
I whipt him for robbing an orchard once when he was but a child –
"The farmer dared me to do it," he said; he was always so wild –
And idle – and couldn't be idle – my Willy – he never could rest.
The King should have made him a soldier, he would have been one
　of his best.

## VII

But he lived with a lot of wild mates, and they never would let him
　be good;
They swore that he dare not rob the mail, and he swore that he
　would;
And he took no life, but he took one purse, and when all was done
He flung it among his fellows – I'll none of it, said my son.

## VIII

I came into court to the Judge and the lawyers. I told them my tale,
God's own truth – but they killed him, they killed him for robbing
　the mail.
They hanged him in chains for a show – we had always borne a
　good name –
To be hanged for a thief – and then put away – isn't that enough
　shame?
Dust to dust – low down – let us hide! but they set him so high
That all the ships of the world could stare at him, passing by.
God 'ill pardon the hell-black raven and horrible fowls of the air,
But not the black heart of the lawyer who killed him and hanged
　him there.

## IX

And the jailer forced me away. I had bid him my last goodbye;
They had fastened the door of his cell. "O mother!" I heard him
　cry.

[70]

I couldn't get back though I tried, he had something further to say,
And now I never shall know it. The jailer forced me away.

### X

Then since I couldn't but hear that cry of my boy that was dead,
They seized me and shut me up: they fastened me down on my bed.
"Mother, O mother!" – he called in the dark to me year after year –
They beat me for that, they beat me – you know that I couldn't but
      hear;
And then at the last they found I had grown so stupid and still
They let me abroad again – but the creatures had worked their will.

### XI

Flesh of my flesh was gone, but bone of my bone was left –
I stole them all from the lawyers – and you, will you call it a theft? –
My baby, the bones that had sucked me, the bones that had laughed
      and had cried –
Theirs? O no! they are mine – not theirs – they had moved in my
      side.

### XII

Do you think I was scared by the bones? I kissed 'em, I buried 'em
      all –
I can't dig deep, I am old – in the night by the churchyard wall.
My Willy 'ill rise up whole when the trumpet of judgment 'ill sound.
But I charge you never to say that I laid him in holy ground.

### XIII

They would scratch him up – they would hang him again on the
      cursèd tree.
Sin? O yes – we are sinners, I know – let all that be,
And read me a Bible verse of the Lord's good will toward men –
"Full of compassion and mercy, the Lord" – let me hear it again;
"Full of compassion and mercy – long-suffering." Yes, O yes!
For the lawyer is born but to murder – the Saviour lives but to bless.
*He'll* never put on the black cap except for the worst of the worst,
And the first may be last – I have heard it in church – and the last
      may be first.
Suffering – O long-suffering – yes, as the Lord must know,
Year after year in the mist and the wind and the shower and the
      snow.

[71]

## XIV

Heard, have you? what? they have told you he never repented his
  sin.
How do they know it? are *they* his mother? are *you* of his kin?
Heard! have you ever heard, when the storm on the downs began,
The wind that 'ill wail like a child and the sea that 'ill moan like
  man?

## XV

Election, Election and Reprobation – it's all very well.
But I go tonight to my boy, and I shall not find him in Hell.
For I cared so much for my boy that the Lord has looked into my
  care,
And He means me I'm sure to be happy with Willy, I know not
  where.

## XVI

And if *he* be lost – but to save *my* soul that is all your desire:
Do you think that I care for *my* soul if my boy be gone to the fire?
I have been with God in the dark – go, go, you may leave me
  alone –
You never have borne a child – you are just as hard as a stone.

## XVII

Madam, I beg your pardon! I think that you mean to be kind,
But I cannot hear what you say for my Willy's voice in the wind –
The snow and the sky so bright – he used but to call in the dark,
And he calls to me now from the church and not from the gibbet –
  for hark!
Nay – you can hear it yourself – it is coming – shaking the walls –
Willy – the moon's in a cloud – Good-night. I am going. He calls.

# WILLIAM BELL SCOTT
## 1811–1890

## *The Witch's Ballad*

O, I hae come from far away,
　From a warm land far away,
A southern land across the sea,
With sailor-lads about the mast,
Merry and canny, and kind to me.

And I hae been to yon town,
　To try my luck in yon town;
Nort, and Mysie, Elspie too.
Right braw we were to pass the gate,
Wi' gowden clasps on girdles blue.

Mysie smiled wi' miminy mouth,
　Innocent mouth, miminy mouth;
Elspie wore her scarlet gown,
Nort's grey eyes were unco' gleg,
My Castile comb was like a crown.

We walked abreast all up the street,
　Into the market up the street;
Our hair with marygolds was wound,
Our bodices with love-knots laced,
Our merchandise with tansy bound.

Nort had chickens, I had cocks,
　Gamesome cocks, loud-crowing cocks;
Mysie ducks, and Elspie drakes, –
For a wee groat or a pound:
We lost nae time wi' gives and takes.

Lost nae time, for well we knew,
　In our sleeves full well we knew,
When the gloaming came that night,
Duck nor drake nor hen nor cock
Would be found by candle-light.

And when our chaffering all was done,
  All was paid for, sold and done,
We drew a glove on ilka hand,
We sweetly curtsied each to each,
And deftly danced a saraband.

The market lasses looked and laughed,
  Left their gear and looked and laughed;
They made as they would join the game,
But soon their mithers, wild and wud,
With whack and screech they stopped the same.

Sae loud the tongues o' randies grew,
  The flitin' and the skirlin' grew,
At all the windows in the place,
Wi' spoons or knives, wi' needle or awl,
Was thrust out every hand and face.

And down each stair they thronged anon,
  Gentle, semple, thronged anon;
Souter and tailer, frowsy Nan,
The ancient widow young again,
Simpering behind her fan.

Without a choice, against their will,
  Doited, dazed, against their will,
The market lassie and her mither,
The farmer and his husbandman,
Hand in hand dance a' thegether.

Slow at first, but faster soon,
  Still increasing wild and fast,
Hoods and mantles, hats and hose,
Blindly doffed and cast away,
Left them naked, heads and toes.

They would have torn us limb from limb,
  Dainty limb from dainty limb;
But never one of them could win
Across the line that I had drawn
With bleeding thumb a-widdershin.

But there was Jeff the provost's son,
  Jeff the provost's only son;
There was Father Auld himsel',
The Lombard frae the hostelry,
And the lawyer Peter Fell.

All goodly men we singled out,
  Waled them well, and singled out,
And drew them by the left hand in;
Mysie the priest, and Elspie won
The Lombard, Nort the lawyer carle,
I mysel' the provost's son.

Then, with cantrip kisses seven,
  Three times round with kisses seven,
Warped and woven there spun we,
Arms and legs and flaming hair,
Like a whirlwind on the sea.

Like the wind that sucks the sea,
  Over and in and on the sea,
Good sooth it was a mad delight;
And every man of all the four
Shut his eyes and laughed outright.

Laughed as long as they had breath,
  Laughed while they had sense or breath;
And close about us coiled a mist
Of gnats and midges, wasps and flies,
Like the whirlwind shaft it rist.

Drawn up I was right off my feet,
  Into the mist and off my feet;
And, dancing on each chimney-top,
I saw a thousand darling imps
Keeping time with skip and hop.

And on the provost's brave ridge-tile,
  On the provost's grand ridge-tile,
The Blackamoor first to master me

I saw, – I saw that winsome smile,
The mouth that did my heart beguile,
And spoke the great Word over me,
In the land beyond the sea.

I called his name, I called aloud,
  Alas! I called on him aloud;
And then he filled his hand with stour,
And threw it towards me in the air;
My mouse flew out, I lost my pow'r!

My lusty strength, my power, were gone;
  Power was gone, and all was gone.
He will not let me love him more!
Of bell and whip and horse's tail
He cares not if I find a store.

But I am proud if he is fierce!
  I am as proud as he is fierce;
I'll turn about and backward go,
If I meet again that Blackamoor,
And he'll help us then, for he shall know
I seek another paramour.

And we'll gang once more to yon town,
  Wi' better luck to yon town;
We'll walk in silk and cramoisie,
And I shall wed the provost's son;
My-lady of the town I'll be!

For I was born a crowned king's child,
  Born and nursed a king's child,
King o' a land ayont the sea,
Where the Blackamoor kissed me first,
And taught me art and glamourie.

Each one in her wame shall hide
  Her hairy mouse, her wary mouse,
Fed on madwort and agramie, –
Wear amber beads between her breasts,
And blind-worm's skin about her knee.

The Lombard shall be Elspie's man,
  Elspie's gowden husband-man;
Nort shall take the lawyer's hand;
The priest shall swear another vow:
We'll dance again the saraband!

# ROBERT BROWNING
## 1812–1889

## *A Woman's Last Word*

### I

Let's contend no more, Love,
  Strive nor weep:
All be as before, Love,
  – Only sleep!

### II

What so wild as words are?
  I and thou
In debate, as birds are,
  Hawk on bough!

### III

See the creature stalking
  While we speak!
Hush and hide the talking,
  Cheek on cheek!

### IV

What so false as truth is,
  False to thee?
Where the serpent's tooth is,
  Shun the tree –

### V

Where the apple reddens
  Never pry –
Lest we lose our Edens,
  Eve and I!

### VI

Be a god and hold me
  With a charm!
Be a man and fold me
  With thine arm!

### VII

Teach me, only teach, Love!
  As I ought
I will speak thy speech, Love,
  Think thy thought –

### VIII

Meet, if thou require it,
  Both demands,
Laying flesh and spirit
  In thy hands.

### IX

That shall be to-morrow
  Not to-night:
I must bury sorrow
  Out of sight:

### X

– Must a little weep, Love,
  (Foolish me!)
And so fall asleep, Love,
  Loved by thee.

## *Any Wife to Any Husband*

### 1

My love, this is the bitterest, that thou –
Who art all truth, and who dost love me now
  As thine eyes say, as thy voice breaks to say –
Should'st love so truly, and could'st love me still
A whole long life through, had but love its will,
  Would death that leads me from thee brook delay!

### 2

I have but to be by thee, and thy hand
Will never let mine go, nor heart withstand
  The beating of my heart to reach its place.
When shall I look for thee and feel thee gone?
When cry for the old comfort and find none?
  Never, I know! Thy soul is in thy face.

[79]

3

Oh, I should fade – 'tis willed so! Might I save,
Gladly I would, whatever beauty gave
    Joy to thy sense, for that was precious too.
It is not to be granted. But the soul
Whence the love comes, all ravage leaves that whole;
    Vainly the flesh fades – soul makes all things new.

4

It would not be because my eye grew dim
Thou could'st not find the love there, thanks to Him
    Who never is dishonoured in the spark
He gave us from his fire of fires, and bade
Remember whence it sprang, nor be afraid
    While that burns on, though all the rest grow dark.

5

So, how thou would'st be perfect, white and clean
Outside as inside, soul and soul's demesne
    Alike, this body given to show it by!
Oh, three-parts through the worst of life's abyss,
What plaudits from the next world after this,
    Could'st thou repeat a stroke and gain the sky!

6

And is it not the bitterer to think
That, disengage our hands and thou wilt sink
    Although thy love was love in very deed?
I know that nature! Pass a festive day,
Thou dost not throw its relic-flower away
    Nor bid its music's loitering echo speed.

7

Thou let'st the stranger's glove lie where it fell;
If old things remain old things all is well,
    For thou art grateful as becomes man best:
And hadst thou only heard me play one tune,
Or viewed me from a window, not so soon
    With thee would such things fade as with the rest.

### 8

I seem to see! We meet and part; 'tis brief:
The book I opened keeps a folded leaf,
   The very chair I sat on, breaks the rank;
That is a portrait of me on the wall –
Three lines, my face comes at so slight a call;
   And for all this, one little hour to thank.

### 9

But now, because the hour through years was fixed,
Because our inmost beings met and mixed,
   Because thou once hast loved me – wilt thou dare
Say to thy soul and Who may list beside,
"Therefore she is immortally my bride,
   Chance cannot change my love, nor time impair.

### 10

"So, what if in the dusk of life that's left,
I, a tired traveller of my sun bereft,
   Look from my path when, mimicking the same,
The fire-fly glimpses past me, come and gone?
– Where was it till the sunset? where anon
   It will be at the sunrise! What's to blame?"

### 11

Is it so helpful to thee? Canst thou take
The mimic up, nor, for the true thing's sake,
   Put gently by such efforts at a beam?
Is the remainder of the way so long,
Thou need'st the little solace, thou the strong?
   Watch out thy watch, let weak ones doze and dream!

### 12

– Ah, but the fresher faces! "Is it true,"
Thoul't ask, "some eyes are beautiful and new?
   Some hair, – how can one choose but grasp such wealth?
And if a man would press his lips to lips
Fresh as the wilding hedge-rose-cup there slips
   The dew-drop out of, must it be by stealth?

### 13

"It cannot change the love still kept for Her,
More than if such a picture I prefer
   Passing a day with, to a room's bare side.
The painted form takes nothing she possessed,
Yet, while the Titian's Venus lies at rest,
   A man looks. Once more, what is there to chide?"

### 14

So must I see, from where I sit and watch,
My own self sell myself, my hand attach
   Its warrant to the very thefts from me –
Thy singleness of soul that made me proud,
Thy purity of heart I love aloud,
   Thy man's-truth I was bold to bid God see!

### 15

Love, so, then, if thou wilt! Give all thou canst
Away to the new faces – disentranced –
   (Say it and think it) obdurate no more,
Re-issue looks and words from the old mint –
Pass them afresh, no matter whose the print
   Image and superscription once they bore!

### 16

Re-coin thyself and give it them to spend, –
It all comes to the same thing at the end,
   Since mine thou wast, mine art, and mine shalt be,
Faithful or faithless, sealing up the sum
Or lavish of my treasure, thou must come
   Back to the heart's place here I keep for thee!

### 17

Only, why should it be with stain at all?
Why must I, 'twixt the leaves of coronal,
   Put any kiss of pardon on thy brow?
Why need the other women know so much,
And talk together, "Such the look and such
   The smile he used to love with, then as now!"

[82]

### 18

Might I die last and shew thee! Should I find
Such hardship in the few years left behind,
  If free to take and light my lamp, and go
Into thy tomb, and shut the door and sit,
Seeing thy face on those four sides of it
  The better that they are so blank, I know!

### 19

Why, time was what I wanted, to turn o'er
Within my mind each look, get more and more
  By heart each word, too much to learn at first,
And join thee all the fitter for the pause
'Neath the low door-way's lintel. That were cause
  For lingering, though thou calledst, if I durst!

### 20

And yet thou art the nobler of us two.
What dare I dream of, that thou canst not do,
  Outstripping my ten small steps with one stride?
I'll say then, here's a trial and a task –
Is it to bear? – if easy, I'll not ask –
  Though love fail, I can trust on in thy pride.

### 21

Pride? – when those eyes forestall the life behind
The death I have to go through! – when I find,
  Now that I want thy help most, all of thee!
What did I fear? Thy love shall hold me fast
Until the little minute's sleep is past
  And I wake saved. – And yet, it will not be!

# EMILY BRONTË
## 1818–1848

## *Song*
## *(The linnet in the rocky dells . . .)*

The linnet in the rocky dells,
The moor-lark in the air,
The bee among the heather-bells
That hide my lady fair:

The wild deer browse above her breast;
The wild birds raise their brood;
And they, her smiles of love caressed,
Have left her solitude!

I ween, that when the grave's dark wall
Did first her form retain,
They thought their hearts could ne'er recall
The light of joy again.

They thought the tide of grief would flow
Unchecked through future years;
But where is all their anguish now,
And where are all their tears?

Well, let them fight for Honour's breath,
Or Pleasure's shade pursue –
The Dweller in the land of Death
Is changed and careless too.

And if their eyes should watch and weep
Till sorrow's source were dry,
She would not, in her tranquil sleep,
Return a single sigh.

Blow, west wind, by the lonely mound,
And murmur, summer streams,
There is no need of other sound
To soothe my Lady's dreams.

# CHRISTINA ROSSETTI
## 1830–1894

## *Amor Mundi*

"Oh where are you going with your love-locks flowing
  On the west wind blowing along this valley track?"
"The downhill path is easy, come with me an it please ye,
  We shall escape the uphill by never turning back."

So they went together in glowing August weather,
  The honey-breathing heather lay to their left and right;
And dear she was to dote on, her swift feet seemed to float on
  The air like soft twin pigeons too sportive to alight.

"Oh what is that in heaven where grey cloud-flakes are seven,
  Where blackest clouds hang riven just at the rainy skirt?"
Oh that's a meteor sent us, a message dumb, portentous,
  An undeciphered solemn signal of help or hurt.

"Oh what is it that glides quickly where velvet flowers grow thickly,
  Their scent comes rich and sickly?" – "A scaled and hooded
    worm."
"Oh what's that in the hollow, so pale I quake to follow?"
  "Oh that's a thin dead body which waits the eternal term."

"Turn again, O my sweetest, – turn again, false and fleetest:
  This beaten way thou beatest I fear is hell's own track."
"Nay, too steep for hill-mounting; nay, too late for cost-counting:
  This downhill path is easy, but there's no turning back."

# JOHN LEICESTER WARREN, LORD DE TABLEY
## 1835–1895

## *Nuptial Song*
## *(Sigh, heart, and break not . . .)*

Sigh, heart, and break not; rest, lark, and wake not!
  Day I hear coming to draw my Love away.
As mere-waves whisper, and clouds grow crisper,
  Ah, like a rose he will waken up with day.

In moon-light lonely, he is my Love only,
  I share with none when Luna rides in grey.
As dawn-beams quicken, my rivals thicken,
  The light and deed and turmoil of the day.

To watch my sleeper to me is sweeter,
  Than any waking words my Love can say;
In dream he finds me and closer winds me!
  Let him rest by me a little more and stay.

Ah, mine eyes, close not; and, tho' he knows not,
  My lips, on his be tender while you may;
Ere leaves are shaken, and ring-doves waken,
  And infant buds begin to scent new day.

Fair Darkness, measure thine hours, as treasure
  Shed each one slowly from thine urn, I pray;
Hoard in and cover each from my lover;
  I cannot lose him yet; dear night, delay.

Each moment dearer, true-love, lie nearer,
  My hair shall blind thee lest thou see the ray;
My locks encumber thine ears in slumber,
  Lest any bird dare give thee note of day.

He rests so calmly; we lie so warmly;
  Hand within hand, as children after play; –
In shafted amber on roof and chamber
  Dawn enters; my Love wakes; here is day.

[86]

# ALGERNON SWINBURNE
## 1837–1909

## *Anactoria*

τίνος αὖ τὺ πειθοὶ
μὰψ σαγηνεύσας φιλότατα;
Sappho

My life is bitter with thy love; thine eyes
Blind me, thy tresses burn me, thy sharp sighs
Divide my flesh and spirit with soft sound,
And my blood strengthens, and my veins abound.
I pray thee sigh not, speak not, draw not breath;
Let life burn down, and dream it is not death.
I would the sea had hidden us, the fire
(Wilt thou fear that, and fear not my desire?)
Severed the bones that bleach, the flesh that cleaves,
And let our sifted ashes drop like leaves.
I feel thy blood against my blood: my pain
Pains thee, and lips bruise lips, and vein stings vein.
Let fruit be crushed on fruit, let flower on flower,
Breast kindle breast, and either burn one hour.
Why wilt thou follow lesser loves? are thine
Too weak to bear these hands and lips of mine?
I charge thee for my life's sake, O too sweet
To crush love with thy cruel faultless feet,
I charge thee keep thy lips from hers or his,
Sweetest, till theirs be sweeter than my kiss:
Lest I too lure, a swallow for a dove,
Erotion or Erinna to my love.
I would my love could kill thee; I am satiated
With seeing thee live, and fain would have thee dead.
I would earth had thy body as fruit to eat,
And no mouth but some serpent's found thee sweet.
I would find grievous ways to have thee slain,
Intense device, and superflux of pain;
Vex thee with amorous agonies, and shake

[87]

Life at thy lips, and leave it there to ache;
Strain out thy soul with pangs too soft to kill,
Intolerable interludes, and infinite ill;
Relapse and reluctation of the breath,
Dumb tunes and shuddering semitones of death.
I am weary of all thy words and soft strange ways,
Of all love's fiery nights and all his days,
And all the broken kisses salt as brine
That shuddering lips make moist with waterish wine,
And eyes the bluer for all those hidden hours
That pleasure fills with tears and feeds from flowers,
Fierce at the heart with fire that half comes through,
But all the flowerlike white stained round with blue;
The fervent underlid, and that above
Lifted with laughter or abashed with love;
Thine amorous girdle, full of thee and fair,
And leavings of the lilies in thine hair.
Yea, all sweet words of thine and all thy ways,
And all the fruit of nights and flower of days,
And stinging lips wherein the hot sweet brine
That Love was born of burns and foams like wine,
And eyes insatiable of amorous hours,
Fervent as fire and delicate as flowers,
Coloured like night at heart, but cloven through
Like night with flame, dyed round like night with blue,
Clothed with deep eyelids under and above –
Yea, all thy beauty sickens me with love;
Thy girdle empty of thee and now not fair,
And ruinous lilies in thy languid hair.
Ah, take no thought for Love's sake; shall this be,
And she who loves thy lover not love thee?
Sweet soul, sweet mouth of all that laughs and lives,
Mine is she, very mine; and she forgives.
For I beheld in sleep the light that is
In her high place in Paphos, heard the kiss
Of body and soul that mix with eager tears
And laughter stinging through the eyes and ears;
Saw Love, as burning flame from crown to feet,
Imperishable, upon her storied seat;

Clear eyelids lifted toward the north and south,
A mind of many colours, and a mouth
Of many tunes and kisses; and she bowed,
With all her subtle face laughing aloud,
Bowed down upon me, saying, "Who doth thee wrong,
Sappho?" but thou – thy body is the song,
Thy mouth the music; thou art more than I,
Though my voice die not till the whole world die;
Though men that hear it madden; though love weep,
Though nature change, though shame be charmed to sleep.
Ah, wilt thou slay me lest I kiss thee dead?
Yet the queen laughed from her sweet heart and said:
"Even she that flies shall follow for thy sake,
And she shall give thee gifts that would not take,
Shall kiss that would not kiss thee" (yea, kiss me)
"When thou wouldst not" – when I would not kiss thee!
Ah, more to me than all men as thou art,
Shall not my songs assuage her at the heart?
Ah, sweet to me as life seems sweet to death,
Why should her wrath fill thee with fearful breath?
Nay, sweet, for is she God alone? hath she
Made earth and all the centuries of the sea,
Taught the sun ways to travel, woven most fine
The moonbeams, shed the starbeams forth as wine,
Bound with her myrtles, beaten with her rods,
The young men and the maidens and the gods?
Have we not lips to love with, eyes for tears,
And summer and flower of women and of years?
Stars for the foot of morning, and for noon
Sunlight, and exaltation of the moon;
Waters that answer waters, fields that wear
Lilies, and languor of the Lesbian air?
Beyond those flying feet of fluttered doves,
Are there not other gods for other loves?
Yea, though she scourge thee, sweetest, for my sake,
Blossom not thorns and flowers not blood should break.
Ah that my lips were tuneless lips, but pressed
To the bruised blossom of thy scourged white breast!
Ah that my mouth for Muses' milk were fed

[89]

On the sweet blood thy sweet small wounds had bled!
That with my tongue I felt them, and could taste
The faint flakes from thy bosom to the waist!
That I could drink thy veins as wine, and eat
Thy breasts like honey! that from face to feet
Thy body were abolished and consumed,
And in my flesh thy very flesh entombed!
Ah, ah, thy beauty! like a beast it bites,
Stings like an adder, like an arrow smites.
Ah sweet, and sweet again, and seven times sweet,
The paces and the pauses of thy feet!
Ah sweeter than all sleep or summer air
The fallen fillets fragrant from thine hair!
Yea, though their alien kisses do me wrong,
Sweeter thy lips than mine with all their song;
Thy shoulders whiter than a fleece of white,
And flower-sweet fingers, good to bruise or bite
As honeycomb of the inmost honey-cells,
With almond-shaped and roseleaf-coloured shells
And blood like purple blossom at the tips
Quivering; and pain made perfect in thy lips
For my sake when I hurt thee; O that I
Durst crush thee out of life with love, and die,
Die of thy pain and my delight, and be
Mixed with thy blood and molten into thee!
Would I not plague thee dying overmuch?
Would I not hurt thee perfectly? not touch
Thy pores of sense with torture, and make bright
Thine eyes with bloodlike tears and grievous light?
Strike pang from pang as note is struck from note,
Catch the sob's middle music in thy throat,
Take thy limbs living, and new-mould with these
A lyre of many faultless agonies?
Feed thee with fever and famine and fine drouth,
With perfect pangs convulse thy perfect mouth,
Make thy life shudder in thee and burn afresh,
And wring thy very spirit through the flesh?
Cruel? but love makes all that love him well
As wise as heaven and crueller than hell.

[90]

Me hath love made more bitter toward thee
Than death toward man; but were I made as he
Who hath made all things to break them one by one,
If my feet trod upon the stars and sun
And souls of men as his have alway trod,
God knows I might be crueller than God.
For who shall change with prayers or thanksgivings
The mystery of the cruelty of things?
Or say what God above all gods and years
With offering and blood-sacrifice of tears,
With lamentation from strange lands, from graves
Where the snake pastures, from scarred mouths of slaves,
From prison, and from plunging prows of ships
Through flamelike foam of the sea's closing lips –
With thwartings of strange signs, and wind-blown hair
Of comets, desolating the dim air,
When darkness is made fast with seals and bars,
And fierce reluctance of disastrous stars,
Eclipse, and sound of shaken hills, and wings
Darkening, and blind inexpiable things –
With sorrow of labouring moons, and altering light
And travail of the planets of the night,
And weeping of the weary Pleiads seven,
Feeds the mute melancholy lust of heaven?
Is not his incense bitterness, his meat
Murder? his hidden face and iron feet
Hath not man known, and felt them on their way
Threaten and trample all things and every day?
Hath he not sent us hunger? who hath cursed
Spirit and flesh with longing? filled with thirst
Their lips who cried unto him? who bade exceed
The fervid will, fall short the feeble deed,
Bade sink the spirit and the flesh aspire,
Pain animate the dust of dead desire,
And yield up her flower to violent fate?
Him would I reach, him smite, him desecrate,
Pierce the cold lips of God with human breath,
And mix his immortality with death.
Why hath he made us? what had all we done

That we should live and loathe the sterile sun,
And with the moon wax paler as she wanes,
And pulse by pulse feel time grow through our veins?
Thee too the years shall cover; thou shalt be
As the rose born of one same blood with thee,
As a song sung, as a word said, and fall
Flower-wise, and be not any more at all,
Nor any memory of thee anywhere;
For never Muse has bound above thine hair
The high Pierian flower whose graft outgrows
All summer kinship of the mortal rose
And colour of deciduous days, nor shed
Reflex and flush of heaven about thine head,
Nor reddened brows made pale by floral grief
With splendid shadow from that lordlier leaf.
Yea, thou shalt be forgotten like spilt wine,
Except these kisses of my lips on thine
Brand them with immortality; but me –
Men shall not see bright fire nor hear the sea,
Nor mix their hearts with music, nor behold
Cast forth of heaven, with feet of awful gold
And plumeless wings that make the bright air blind,
Lightning, with thunder for a hound behind
Hunting through fields unfurrowed and unsown,
But in the light and laughter, in the moan
And music, and in grasp of lip and hand
And shudder of water that makes felt on land
The immeasurable tremor of all the sea,
Memories shall mix and metaphors of me.
Like me shall be the shuddering calm of night,
When all the winds of the world for pure delight
Close lips that quiver and fold up wings that ache
When nightingales are louder for love's sake,
And leaves tremble like lute-strings or like fire;
Like me the one star swooning with desire
Even at the cold lips of the sleepless moon,
As I at thine; like me the waste white noon,
Burnt through with barren sunlight; and like me
The land-stream and the tide-stream in the sea.
I am sick with time as these with ebb and flow,

And by the yearning in my veins I know
The yearning sound of waters; and mine eyes
Burn as that beamless fire which fills the skies
With troubled stars and travailing things of flame;
And in my heart the grief consuming them
Labours, and in my veins the thirst of these,
And all the summer travail of the trees
And all the winter sickness; and the earth,
Filled full with deadly works of death and birth,
Sore spent with hungry lusts of birth and death,
Has pain like mine in her divided breath;
Her spring of leaves is barren, and her fruit
Ashes; her boughs are burdened, and her root
Fibrous and gnarled with poison; underneath
Serpents have gnawn it through with tortuous teeth
Made sharp upon the bones of all the dead,
And wild birds rend her branches overhead.
These, woven as raiment for his word and thought,
These hath God made, and me as these, and wrought
Song, and hath lit it at my lips; and me
Earth shall not gather though she feed on thee.
As a shed tear shalt thou be shed; but I –
Lo, earth may labour, men live long and die,
Years change and stars, and the high God devise
New things, and old things wane before his eyes
Who wields and wrecks them, being more strong than they –
But, having made me, me he shall not slay.
Nor slay nor satiate, like those herds of his
Who laugh and live a little, and their kiss
Contents them, and their loves are swift and sweet,
And sure death grasps and gains them with slow feet,
Love they or hate they, strive or bow their knees –
And all these end; he hath his will of these.
Yea, but albeit he slay me, hating me –
Albeit he hide me in the deep dear sea
And cover me with cool wan foam, and ease
This soul of mine as any soul of these,
And give me water and great sweet waves, and make
The very sea's name lordlier for my sake,
The whole sea sweeter – albeit I die indeed

And hide myself and sleep and no man heed,
Of me the high God hath not all his will.
Blossom of branches, and on each high hill
Clear air and wind, and under in clamours vales
Fierce noises of the fiery nightingales,
Buds burning in the sudden spring like fire,
The wan washed sand and the waves' vain desire,
Sails seen like blown white flowers at sea, and words
That bring tears swiftest, and long notes of birds
Violently singing till the whole world sings –
I Sappho shall be one with all these things,
With all high things for ever; and my face
Seen once, my songs once heard in a strange place,
Cleave to men's lives, and waste the days thereof
With gladness and much sadness and long love.
Yea, they shall say, earth's womb has borne in vain
New things, and never this best thing again;
Borne days and men, borne fruits and wars and wine,
Seasons and songs, but no song more like mine.
And they shall know me as ye who have known me here,
Last year when I loved Atthis, and this year
When I love thee; and they shall praise me, and say
"She hath all time as all we have our day,
Shall she not live and have her will" – even I?
Yea, though thou diest, I say I shall not die.
For these shall give me of their souls, shall give
Life, and the days and loves wherewith I live,
Shall quicken me with loving, fill with breath,
Save me and serve me, strive for me with death.
Alas, that neither moon nor snow nor dew
Nor all cold things can purge me wholly through,
Assuage me nor allay me nor appease,
Till supreme sleep shall bring me bloodless ease;
Till time wax faint in all his periods;
Till fate undo the bondage of the gods,
And lay, to slake and satiate me all through,
Lotus and Lethe on my lips like dew,
And shed around and over and under me
Thick darkness and the insuperable sea.

# MARY E. TUCKER
## 1838?–?

## *Crazed*

No rest! no rest on this bleak earth for me;
  A thousand fancies flit across my brain;
Dim phantoms of the shadowy past I see –
  I know, oh God! I know I am insane.

Deep in my breast the secret I will hide –
  To those who love me 'twould give bitter pain:
Foes would rejoice should evil ere betide,
  And 'tis an awful curse to be insane.

Ho! ho! a light! I say, my wife, a light!
  This heavy darkness crushes my poor heart;
And, darling, sit beside my bed to-night –
  Thy kind words comfort to my soul impart.

Ah, do not start, when my deep groans you hear:
  I stagger, struck with agony so fell;
See there! see there! 'tis gone; you need not fear;
  You cannot see the Devil's mystic spell.

I hear a footstep! Halt! I say, who's there?
  The wind, you answer; ah, I'm not insane!
You can't deceive me with your words so fair –
  There! there! I hear the sound approach again.

The light! I say! I tell you I will see –
  It is a thief, with murderous thought intent;
You can't prevent me – but, ah, woe is me!
  Are you, too, on some hidden mischief bent?

Forgive me, darling; I did wildly rave;
  I think I am a little crazed tonight.
Stay with me, pet-wife, you are good and brave;
  The spell will pass with morning's dawning bright.

Press your soft hand upon my aching head –
  Weeping again? Why will you always weep?
Your eyes their brightness with the tears will shed: .
  There, good night, darling! now, I fain would sleep.

[95]

# THOMAS HARDY
## 1840–1928

## *Circus-Rider to Ringmaster*

When I am riding round the ring no longer,
    Tell a tale of me;
Say, no steed-borne woman's nerve was stronger
    Than mine used to be.
  Let your whole soul say it; do:
    O it will be true!

Should I soon no more be mistress found in
    Feats I've made my own,
Trace the tan-laid track you'd whip me round in
    On the cantering roan:
  There may cross your eyes again
    My lithe look as then.

Show how I, when clay becomes my cover,
    Took the high-hoop leap
Into your arms, who coaxed and grew my lover, –
    Ah, to make me weep
  Since those claspings cared for so
    Ever so long ago!

Though not now as when you freshly knew me,
    But a fading form,
Shape the kiss you'd briskly blow up to me
    While our love was warm,
  And my cheek unstained by tears,
    As in these last years!

# ALICE MEYNELL
## 1847–1922

## *The Shepherdess*

She walks – the lady of my delight –
  A shepherdess of sheep.
Her flocks are thoughts. She keeps them white;
  She guards them from the steep;
She feeds them on the fragrant height,
  And folds them in for sleep.

She roams maternal hills and bright,
  Dark valleys safe and deep.
Into that tender breast at night
  The chastest stars may peep.
She walks – the lady of my delight –
  A shepherdess of sheep.

She holds her little thoughts in sight,
  Though gay they run and leap.
She is so circumspect and right;
  She has her soul to keep.
She walks – the lady of my delight –
  A shepherdess of sheep.

# LOUISE IMOGEN GUINEY
## 1861–1920

## *The Wild Ride*

I hear in my heart, I hear in its ominous pulses
All day, on the road, the hoofs of invisible horses,
All night, from their stalls, the importunate pawing and neighing.

Let cowards and laggards fall back! but alert to the saddle
Weather-worn and abreast, go men of our galloping legion,
With a stirrup-cup each to the lily of women that loves him.

The trail is through dolour and dread, over crags and morasses;
There are shapes by the way, there are things that appal or entice
     us:
What odds? We are Knights of the Grail, we are vowed to the
     riding.

Thought's self is a vanishing wing, and joy is a cobweb,
And friendship a flower in the dust, and glory a sunbeam:
Not here is our prize, nor, alas! after these our pursuing.

A dipping of plumes, a tear, a shake of the bridle,
A passing salute to this world and her pitiful beauty:
We hurry with never a word in the track of our fathers.

(I hear in my heart, I hear in its ominous pulses
All day, on the road, the hoofs of invisible horses,
All night, from their stalls, the importunate pawing and neighing.)

We spur to a land of no name, out-racing the storm-wind;
We leap to the infinite dark like sparks from the anvil.
Thou leadest, O God! All's well with Thy troopers that follow.

# The Knight Errant

## (Donatello's Saint George)

Spirits of old that bore me,
And set me, meek of mind,
Between great dreams before me,
And deeds as great behind,
Knowing humanity my star
As first abroad I ride,
Shall help me wear with every scar
Honour at eventide.

Let claws of lightning clutch me
From summer's groaning cloud,
Or ever malice touch me,
And glory make me proud.
Oh, give my youth, my faith, my sword,
Choice of the heart's desire:
A short life in the saddle, Lord!
Not long life by the fire.

Forethought and recollection
Rivet mine armour gay!
The passion for perfection
Redeem my failing way!
The arrow of the upper slope
From sudden ambush cast,
Rain quick and true, with one to ope
My Paradise at last!

I fear no breathing bowman,
But only, east and west,
The awful other foeman
Impowered in my breast.
The outer fray in the sun shall be,
The inner beneath the moon;
And may Our Lady lend to me
Sight of the Dragon soon!

# AMY LEVY
## 1861–1889

## *In the Mile End Road*

How like her! But 'tis she herself,
  Comes up the crowded street!
How little did I think, this morn,
  My only love to meet!

Who else that motion and that mien?
  Whose else that airy tread?
For one strange moment I forgot
  My only love was dead.

# RUDYARD KIPLING
## 1865–1936

## *Harp Song of the Dane Women*

What is a woman that you forsake her,
And the hearth-fire and the home-acre,
To go with the old grey Widow-maker?

She has no house to lay a guest in –
But one chill bed for all to rest in,
That the pale suns and the stray bergs nest in.

She has no strong white arms to fold you,
But the ten-time-fingering weed to hold you –
Out on the rocks where the tide has rolled you.

Yet, when the signs of summer thicken,
And the ice breaks, and the birch-buds quicken,
Yearly you turn from our side, and sicken –

Sicken again for the shouts and the slaughters.
You steal away to the lapping waters,
And look at your ship in her winter-quarters.

You forget our mirth, and talk at the tables,
The kine of the shed and the horse in the stables –
To pitch her sides and go over her cables.

Then you drive out where the storm-clouds swallow,
And the sound of your oar-blades, falling hollow,
Is all that we have left through the months to follow.

Ah, what is Woman that you forsake her,
And the hearth-fire and the home-acre,
To go with the old grey Widow-maker?

# WILLIAM BUTLER YEATS
## 1865–1939

## *Crazy Jane On God*

That lover of a night
Came when he would,
Went in the dawning light
Whether I would or no;
Men come, men go,
*All things remain in God.*

Banners choke the sky;
Men-at-arms tread;
Armoured horses neigh
Where the great battle was
In the narrow pass:
*All things remain in God.*

Before their eyes a house
That from childhood stood
Uninhabited, ruinous,
Suddenly lit up
From door to top:
*All things remain in God.*

I had wild Jack for a lover;
Though like a road
That men pass over
My body makes no groan
But sings on;
*All things remain in God.*

# RICHARD LE GALLIENNE
## 1866–1947

## *Beauty Accurst*

I am so fair that wheresoe'er I wend
  Men yearn with strange desire to kiss my face,
Stretch out their hands to touch me as I pass,
  And women follow me from place to place.

A poet writing honey of his dear
  Leaves the wet page, – ah!, leaves it long to dry.
The bride forgets it is her marriage morn,
  The bridegroom too forgets as I go by.

Within the street where my strange feet shall stray
  All markets hush and traffickers forget,
In my gold head forget their meaner gold,
  The poor man grows unmindful of his debt.

Two lovers kissing in a secret place,
  Should I draw nigh, – will never kiss again;
I come between the king and his desire,
  And where I am all loving else is vain.

Lo! when I walk along the woodland way
  Strange creatures leer at me with uncouth love
And from the grass reach upward to my breast,
  And to my mouth lean from the boughs above.

The sleepy kine move round me in desire
  And press their oozy lips upon my hair,
Toads kiss my feet and creatures of the mire,
  The snails will leave their shells to watch me there.

But all this worship, what is it to me?
  I smite the ox and crush the toad to death:
I only know I am so very fair,
  And that the world was made to give me breath.

[103]

I only wait the hour when God shall rise
   Up from the star where he so long hath sat,
And bow before the wonder of my eyes
   And set *me* there – I am so fair as that.

# EDGAR LEE MASTERS
## 1869–1930

## *Jennie McGrew*

NOT, where the stairway turns in the dark,
A hooded figure, shriveled under a flowing cloak!
Not yellow eyes in the room at night,
Staring out from a surface of cobweb gray!
And not the flap of a condor wing,
When the roar of life in your ears begins
As a sound heard never before!
But on a sunny afternoon,
By a country road,
Where purple rag-weeds bloom along a straggling fence,
And the field is gleaned, and the air is still,
To see against the sun-light something black,
Like a blot with an iris rim –
That is the sign to eyes of second sight . . .
And that I saw!

## *Margaret Fuller Slack*

I would have been as great as George Eliot
But for an untoward fate.
For look at the photograph of me made by Penniwit,
Chin resting on hand, and deep-set eyes –
Gray, too, and far-searching.
But there was the old, old problem:
Should it be celibacy, matrimony or unchastity?
Then John Slack, the rich druggist, wooed me,
Luring me with the promise of leisure for my novel.
And I married him, giving birth to eight children,
And had no time to write.
It was all over with me, anyway,
When I ran the needle in my hand
While washing the baby's things,
And died from lock-jaw, an ironical death.
Hear me, ambitious souls,
Sex is the curse of life!

# CHARLOTTE MEW
## 1869–1928

## *The Farmer's Bride*

Three summers since I chose a maid,
  Too young maybe – but more's to do
At harvest-time than bide and woo.
  When us was wed she turned afraid
Of love and me and all things human;
Like the shut of a winter's day
Her smile went out, and 'twadn't a woman –
  More like a little frightened fay.
    One night, in the Fall, she runned away.

"Out 'mong the sheep, her be," they said,
Should properly have been abed;
But sure enough she wadn't there
Lying awake with her wide brown stare.
So over seven-acre field and up-along across the down
  We chased her, flying like a hare
Before our lanterns. To Church-Town
  All in a shiver and a scare
We caught her, fetched her home at last
  And turned the key upon her, fast.

She does the work about the house
As well as most, but like a mouse:
  Happy enough to chat and play
  With birds and rabbits and such as they,
  So long as men-folk keep away.

"Not near, not near!" her eyes beseech
When one of us comes within reach.
  The women say that beasts in a stall
  Look round like children at her call.
  I've hardly heard her speak at all.

Shy as a leveret, swift as he,
Straight and slight as a young larch tree,

[107]

Sweet as the first wild violets, she,
To her wild self. But what to me?

The short days shorten and the oaks are brown,
   The blue smoke rises to the low grey sky,
One leaf in the still air falls slowly down,
   A magpie's spotted feathers lie
On the black earth spread white with rime,
The berries redden up to Christmas-time.
   What's Christmas-time without there be
   Some other in the house than we!
   She sleeps up in the attic there
   Alone, poor maid. 'Tis but a stair
Betwixt us. Oh! my God! the down,
The soft young down of her, the brown,
The brown of her – her eyes, her hair, her hair!

# ROBERT FROST
## 1874–1963

# *The Hill Wife*

## I. Loneliness

### *Her Word*

One ought not to have to care
  So much as you and I
Care when the birds come round the house
  To seem to say good-by;

Or care so much when they come back
  With whatever it is they sing;
The truth being we are as much
  Too glad for the one thing

As we are too sad for the other here –
  With birds that fill their breasts
But with each other and themselves
  And their built or driven nests.

## II. House Fear

Always – I tell you this they learned –
Always at night when they returned
To the lonely house from far away,
To lamps unlighted and fire gone gray,
They learned to rattle the lock and key
To give whatever might chance to be,
Warning and time to be off in flight:
And preferring the out- to the indoor night,
They learned to leave the house door wide
Until they had lit the lamp inside.

## III. The Smile

### Her Word

I didn't like the way he went away.
That smile! It never came of being gay.
Still he smiled – did you see him? – I was sure!
Perhaps because we gave him only bread
And the wretch knew from that that we were poor.
Perhaps because he let us give instead
Of seizing from us as he might have seized.
Perhaps he mocked at us for being wed,
Or being very young (and he was pleased
To have a vision of us old and dead).
I wonder how far down the road he's got.
He's watching from the woods as like as not.

## IV. The Oft-Repeated Dream

She had no saying dark enough
   For the dark pine that kept
Forever trying the window latch
   Of the room where they slept.

The tireless but ineffectual hands
   That with every futile pass
Made the great tree seem as a little bird
   Before the mystery of glass!

It never had been inside the room,
   And only one of the two
Was afraid in an oft-repeated dream
   Of what the tree might do.

## V. The Impulse

It was too lonely for her there,
   And too wild,
And since there were but two of them,
   And no child,

And work was little in the house,
  She was free,
And followed where he furrowed field,
  Or felled tree.

She rested on a log and tossed
  The fresh chips,
With a song only to herself
  On her lips.

And once she went to break a bough
  Of black alder.
She strayed so far she scarcely heard
  When he called her –

And didn't answer – didn't speak –
  Or return.
She stood, and then she ran and hid
  In the fern.

He never found her, though he looked
  Everywhere,
And he asked at her mother's house
  Was she there.

Sudden and swift and light as that
  The ties gave,
And he learned of finalities
  Besides the grave.

# WALLACE STEVENS
## 1876–1955

## *The Plot Against the Giant*

### First Girl

When this yokel comes maundering,
Whetting his hacker,
I shall run before him,
Diffusing the civilest odors
Out of the geraniums and unsmelled flowers.
It will check him.

### Second Girl

I shall run before him,
Arching cloths besprinkled with colors
As small as fish-eggs.
The threads
Will abash him.

### Third Girl

Oh, la . . . le pauvre!
I shall run before him,
With a curious puffing.
He will bend his ear then.
I shall whisper
Heavenly labials in a world of gutturals.
It will undo him.

# PRISCILLA JANE THOMPSON
## 1882-?

## *The Favorite Slave's Story*

Well, son de story of my life,
   Is long, and full of shade;
And yet, the bright spots, here and tha,
   A heap of comforts made.

When fust my eyes beheld de light,
   'Twas on a Chris'mus day;
Twelve miles fum Richmond "on a fa'm,"
   As you young upsta'ts say.

We said "plantation" in de South,
   We black, and white folks too;
We wa'n't a changin' ev'ry day,
   Like all you young folks do.

My mother cooked de white-folks grub,
   Dat's all she had to do,
Ole Miss, she spilte her half to death,
   And spilte her young ones, too.

Fah, well I mind me, in dem days,
   How I and Sue and Pete,
Would roll around Miss Nancy's cheer,
   And play about her feet.

Miss Nancy, – I kin hear her yet –
   "You Petah, Sue an' Si!
I'll make yo' maustah whoop you sho!"
   (Wid laughtah in her eye.)

Ole mause, he'd whoop us soon as not;
   But, when Miss Nancy saw,
She'd run out, wid dat look, an' say,
   "I wouldn't whoop him, Pa."

One day, – I nevah kin fahgit,
    Ole Miss wus sick in bed;
Ole Mause, he ripped, an' cussed, an' to',
    An' made himself a dread.

Somehow, I can't tell how it wus,
    He slapped my sistah Sue,
And mammy, coase she took it up,
    Den dah wus heap to do.

Pete lit right in wid tooth and claw,
    And so did little sis,
Fah me, I had anothah plan,
    I flew upstairs fah Miss.

I met Miss Nancy on de stairs,
    Wrapped in a great big shawl,
An' comin' down de steps so fast,
    Jest seemed as ef she'd fall.

I tried to tell her "whut wus up,"
    She pushed me on befo',
Fah mammy's cries wus in her yeahs,
    An' she heard nothin' mo'.

She caught ole Mause, an' pulled him off;
    Her eyes dey fa'ly blazed;
Ole Mause commenced a silly grin,
    An' looked like he wus dazed.

I'd nevah seed Miss Nancy mad,
    Good L'od! She fussed an' to'e;
She raked ole Maustah o'er de coals,
    Until he begged an' swo'.

                    * * *

An' aftah dat, I tell you, son,
    Ole Mause, he let us be,
An' doe he slashed de othah slaves,
    Pete, Sue, an' me went free.

An' so de time went spinnin' on,
  Wid not a keer nor plan;
I didn't know whut trouble wus,
  Till I wus nigh a man.

Ole Fairfax owned my fathah, son,
  Dey lived across de creek,
De white folks al'ays let him come,
  Three nights in ev'ry week.

Of coase he had his Sundays, too,
  Great days dey use to be,
Fah all de blessed day he'd have,
  We young ones, bout his knee.

Or else, he'd take us all to church,
  All breshed up neat an' new,
Wid Mammy hanging to his arm,
  An' leading little Sue.

An' Mammy's eyes 'ud be so bright,
  When she had Pappy near;
She'd laugh an' giggle like a gal,
  But tryin' times drawed near.

Ole Mause an' Fairfax wus fast friends;
  A pa' uv roscals dey;
In gamblin', cheatin', an' de like,
  Dey bofe had heap to say.

So bofe got mixed up in a scrape,
  Wid Richmond's bank, an' den,
Dey bofe sold ev'ry slave dey had,
  To keep out uv de pen.

I tell you son de good white-folks,
  Wus good in time uv ease;
But soon as hawd times cummed tha' way,
  Dey'd change, "quick as you please."

Soon as Miss Nancy seed de trap,
  Ole Mause had done walked in,
She changed right dah, an who but she!
  A-helpin' him to sin.

Dey talked an' planned togethah, long;
  An', as de days flew by,
Miss Nancy changed an' got so cross,
  Dat Mammy use to cry.

One mawnin', jest to pick a fuss,
  She said she missed a pie;
When Mammy said dey all wus tha,
  She said, she told a lie.

"Dat pie wus in her cabin, hid;
  She wus a vixen, bold;
An' ef she didn't bring it back,
  She'd have her whooped an' sold."

Well, son, you see dat wus her scheme,
  To see her, wid de rest;
An' aftah dat, she made it plain,
  To all uv us, I 'fess.

An' so, at last, de day rolled 'round,
  When all, exceptin' I,
Wus put upon de block an' sold,
  To any one who'd buy.

Oh, son! You don't know whut it is,
  To see yo' loved ones sold,
An' hear de groans, an' see de tears,
  Uv young, as well as ole.

An' see dem white men bus'lin 'roun',
  A-feelin' uv yo' a'm,
An' havin' you to run an' skip,
  An' caper till you's wa'm,

An' all de while, wid questions, keen,
  An' wid a watchful eye,
Not keerin' how yo' h'a't might ache,
  Jest so you's strong an' spry.

Po' Mammy! How kin I fahgit,
  Her pa'tin' from us all?
Dat pa'tin', son, will 'bide wid me,
  Until de Lo'd will call!

\* \* \*

Ah well! De sun will sometimes shine,
  E'en in a po' slave's life;
De Lo'd healed up my broken h'a't,
  By sendin' me a wife.

Miss Nancy wus as good to her,
  An' spilte her jest as bad,
As she did mammy long befo',
  Sometimes it made me sad.

Ole Mause had prospered, bought mo' slaves,
  Ole Miss wus sweet an' kind,
My little ones an' Charlotte dear,
  Had pushed my grief behind.

I al'ays wus Miss Nancy's pet,
  She made it very plain;
An' I must say, in all my grief,
  She tried to ease my pain.

An' now, dat I wus gay once mo',
  An' happy as could be,
She petted Charlotte an' my chaps,
  An' seemed as pleased as me.

So time sped on widout a keer,
  Save whut had long since past,
Till Ole Mause's health begin to fail,
  An' son, he went down fast.

\* \* \*

De wah, dat had been grumblin' roun',
  Broke full about dis time,
De slaves begun a-walkin' off,
  To suit their own free mind.

Ole Miss wus cryin' day an' night,
   An' beggin' me to stay,
While Charlotte urged me, on de sly,
   To go North, fah away.

I looked into her pleadin' eyes,
   So helpless, trustin' me,
An' den, upon my little chaps,
   An' manhood said, "Be free!"

Ole Missus cumed down to de gate;
   To bid fahwell she tried,
But she jest held fast bofe our hands,
   An' cried, an' cried, an' cried.

An' so we cumed up to dis state,
   An' worked on, bes' we could,
A-trustin' al'ays in de Lo'd,
   An' tryin' to be good.

# FANNIE STEARNS GIFFORD
## 1884-?

## *Moon Folly*

### (from "The Songs of Conn the Fool")

I will go up the mountain after the Moon:
She is caught in a dead fir-tree.
Like a great pale apple of silver and pearl,
Like a great pale apple is she.

I will leap and will catch her with quick cold hands
And carry her home in my sack.
I will set her down safe on the oaken bench
That stands at the chimney-back.

And then I will sit by the fire all night,
And sit by the fire all day.
I will gnaw at the Moon to my heart's delight
Till I gnaw her slowly away.

And while I grow mad with the Moon's cold taste
The World will beat at my door,
Crying "Come out!" and crying "Make haste,
And give us the Moon once more!"

But I shall not answer them ever at all.
I shall laugh, as I count and hide
The great black beautiful Seeds of the Moon
In a flower-pot deep and wide.

Then I shall lie down and go fast asleep,
Drunken with flame and aswoon.
But the seeds will sprout and the seeds will leap,
The subtle swift seeds of the Moon.

And some day, all of the World that cries
And beats at my door shall see
A thousand moon-leaves spring from my thatch
On a wonderful white Moon-tree!

Then each shall have Moons to his heart's desire:
Apples of silver and pearl;
Apples of orange and copper fire
Setting his five wits aswirl!

And then they will thank me, who mock me now,
"Wanting the Moon is he," –
Oh, I'm off to the mountain after the Moon,
Ere she falls from the dead fir-tree!

## EZRA POUND
### 1885–1972

# *The River Merchant's Wife: A Letter*

While my hair was still cut straight across my forehead
Played I about the front gate, pulling flowers.
You came by on bamboo stilts, playing horse,
You walked about my seat, playing with blue plums.
And we went on living in the village of Chōkan:
Two small people, without dislike or suspicion.

At fourteen I married My Lord you.
I never laughed, being bashful.
Lowering my head, I looked at the wall.
Called to, a thousand times, I never looked back.

At fifteen I stopped scowling,
I desired my dust to be mingled with yours
Forever and forever and forever.
Why should I climb the look out?

At sixteen you departed,
You went into far Ku-tō-en, by the river of swirling eddies,
And you have been gone five months.
The monkeys make sorrowful noise overhead.

You dragged your feet when you went out.
By the gate now, the moss is grown, the different mosses,
Too deep to clear them away!
The leaves fall early this autumn, in wind.
The paired butterflies are already yellow with August
Over the grass in the West garden;
They hurt me. I grow older.
If you are coming down through the narrows of the River Kiang,
Please let me know beforehand,
And I will come out to meet you
    As far as Chō-fū-Sa.

*By Rihaku (Li T'ai Po)*

# H.D.
## 1886–1961

## *Hippolytus Temporizes*

I worship the greatest first –
(it were sweet, the couch,
the brighter ripple of cloth
over the dipped fleece;
the thought: her bones
under the flesh are white
as sand which along a beach
covers but keeps the print
of the crescent shapes beneath:
I thought:
between cloth and fleece,
so her body lies.)

I worship first, the great –
(ah, sweet, your eyes –
what God, invoked in Crete,
gave them the gift to part
as the Sidonian myrtle-flower
suddenly, wide and swart,
then swiftly,
the eye-lids having provoked our hearts --
as suddenly beat and close.)

I worship the feet, flawless,
that haunt the hills –
(ah, sweet, dare I think,
beneath the fetter of golden clasp,
of the rhythm, the fall and rise
of yours, carven, slight
beneath the straps of gold that keep
their slender beauty caught,
like wings and bodies
of trapped birds.)

I worship the greatest first –
(suddenly into my brain –
the flash of sun on the snow,
the fringe of light and the drift,
the crest and the hill-shadow –
ah, surely now I forget,
ah splendour, my goddess turns:
or was it the sudden heat,
beneath quivering of molten flesh,
of veins, purple as violets?)

# FENTON JOHNSON
## 1888–1958

## *The Scarlet Woman*

Once I was good like the Virgin Mary and the Minister's wife.
My father worked for Mr. Pullman and white people's tips; but he
    died two days after his insurance expired.
I had nothing, so I had to go to work.
All the stock I had was a white girl's education and a face that
    enchanted the men of both races.
Starvation danced with me.
So when Big Lizzie, who kept a house for white men, came to me
    with tales of fortune that I could reap from the sale of my
    virtue I bowed my head to Vice.
Now I can drink more gin than any man for miles around.
Gin is better than all the water in Lethe.

CLAUDE McKAY

# CLAUDE McKAY
## 1890–1948

## *The Wild Goat*

O you would clothe me in silken frocks
  And house me from the cold,
And bind with bright bands my glossy locks,
  And buy me chains of gold.

And give me, meekly to do my will,
  The hapless sons of men;
But the wild goat bounding on the barren hill
  Droops in the grassy pen.

# EDNA ST. VINCENT MILLAY
## 1892–1950

## *Menses*
## *(He speaks, but to himself, being aware*
## *how it is with her)*

Think not I have not heard.
Well-fanged the double word
And well-directed flew.

I felt it. Down my side
Innocent as oil I see the ugly venom slide:
Poison enough to stiffen us both, and all our friends;
But I am not pierced, so there the mischief ends.

There is more to be said; I see it coiling;
The impact will be pain.
Yet coil; yet strike again.
You cannot riddle the stout mail I wove
Long since, of wit and love.

As for my answer . . . stupid in the sun
He lies, his fangs drawn:
I will not war with you.

You know how wild you are. You are willing to be turned
To other matters; you would be grateful, even.
You watch me shyly. I (for I have learned
More things than one in our few years together)
Chafe at the churlish wind, the unseasonable weather.

"Unseasonable?" you cry, with harsher scorn
Than the theme warrants; "Every year it is the same!
'Unseasonable' they whine, these stupid peasants! – and never
    since they were born
Have they known a spring less wintry! Lord, the shame,
The crying shame of seeing a man no wiser than the beasts he feeds –
His skull as empty as a shell!"

("Go to. You are unwell.")

Such is my thought, but such are not my words.

"What is the name," I ask, "of those big birds
With yellow breast and low and heavy flight,
That make such mournful whistling?"

                                 "Meadowlarks,"
You answer primly, not a little cheered.
"Some people shoot them." Suddenly your eyes are wet
And your chin trembles. On my breast you lean,
And sob most pitifully for all the lovely things that are not and have
    been.

"How silly I am! – and I *know* how silly I am!"
You say; "You are very patient. You are very kind.
I shall be better soon. Just heaven consign and damn
To tedious Hell this body with its muddy feet in my mind!"

# LOUISE BOGAN
## 1897–1970

## *The Crossed Apple*

I've come to give you fruit from out of my orchard,
Of wide report.
I have trees there that bear me many apples
Of every sort;

Clear, streakèd; red and russet; green and golden;
Sour and sweet.
This apple's from a tree yet unbeholden,
Where two kinds meet, –

So that this side is red without a dapple,
And this side's hue
Is clear and snowy. It's a lovely apple.
It is for you.

Within are five black pips as big as peas,
As you will find,
Potent to breed you five great apple trees
Of varying kind:

To breed you wood for fire, leaves for shade,
Apples for sauce.
Oh, this is a good apple for a maid,
It is a cross,

Fine on the finer, so the flesh is tight,
And grained like silk.
Sweet Burning gave the red side, and the white
Is Meadow Milk.

Eat it; and you will taste more than the fruit:
The blossom, too,
The sun, the air, the darkness at the root,
The rain, the dew,

The earth we came to, and the time we flee,
The fire and the breast.
I claim the white part, maiden, that's for me.
You take the rest.

# LANGSTON HUGHES
## 1902–1967

## *Madam and Her Madam*

I worked for a woman,
She wasn't mean –
But she had a twelve-room
House to clean.

Had to get breakfast,
Dinner, and supper, too –
Then take care of her children
When I got through.

Wash, iron, and scrub,
Walk the dog around –
It was too much,
Nearly broke me down.

I said, Madam,
Can it be
You trying to make a
Pack-horse out of me?

She opened her mouth.
She cried, Oh, no!
You know, Alberta,
I love you so!

I said, Madam,
That may be true –
But I'll be dogged
If I love you!

# W.H. AUDEN
## 1907–1973

## *Miranda*

*(excerpted from "The Sea and the Mirror")*

My Dear One is mine as mirrors are lonely,
As the poor and sad are real to the good king,
And the high green hill sits always by the sea.

Up jumped the Black Man behind the elder tree,
Turned a somersault and ran away waving;
My Dear One is mine as mirrors are lonely.

The Witch gave a squawk; her venomous body
Melted into light as water leaves a spring
And the high green hill sits always by the sea.

At his crossroads, too, the Ancient prayed for me;
Down his wasted cheeks tears of joy were running:
My Dear One is mine as mirrors are lonely.

He kissed me awake, and no one was sorry;
The sun shone on sails, eyes, pebbles, anything,
And the high green hill sits always by the sea.

So, to remember our changing garden, we
Are linked as children in a circle dancing:
My Dear One is mine as mirrors are lonely,
And the high green hill sits always by the sea.

# THEODORE ROETHKE
## 1908–1963

## *Her Reticence*

If I could send him only
One sleeve with my hand in it,
Disembodied, unbloody,
For him to kiss or caress
As he would or would not, –
But never the full look of my eyes,
Nor the whole heart of my thought,
Nor the soul haunting my body,
Nor my lips, my breasts, my thighs
That shiver in the wind
When the wind sighs.

# ELIZABETH BISHOP
## 1911–1979

## *Crusoe in England*

A new volcano has erupted,
the papers say, and last week I was reading
where some ship saw an island being born:
at first a breath of steam, ten miles away;
and then a black fleck – basalt, probably –
rose in the mate's binoculars
and caught on the horizon like a fly.
They named it. But my poor old island's still
un-rediscovered, un-renamable.
None of the books has ever got it right.

Well, I had fifty-two
miserable, small volcanoes I could climb
with a few slithery strides –
volcanoes dead as ash heaps.
I used to sit on the edge of the highest one
and count the others standing up,
naked and leaden, with their heads blown off.
I'd think that if they were the size
I thought volcanoes should be, then I had
become a giant;
and if I had become a giant,
I couldn't bear to think what size
the goats and turtles were,
or the gulls, or the overlapping rollers
– a glittering hexagon of rollers
closing and closing in, but never quite,
glittering and glittering, though the sky
was mostly overcast.

My island seemed to be
a sort of cloud-dump. All the hemisphere's
left-over clouds arrived and hung
above the craters – their parched throats
were hot to touch.

Was that why it rained so much?
And why sometimes the whole place hissed?
The turtles lumbered by, high-domed,
hissing like teakettles.
(And I'd have given years, or taken a few,
for any sort of kettle, of course.)
The folds of lava, running out to sea,
would hiss. I'd turn. And then they'd prove
to be more turtles.
The beaches were all lava, variegated,
black, red, and white, and gray;
the marbled colors made a fine display.
And I had waterspouts. Oh,
half a dozen at a time, far out,
they'd come and go, advancing and retreating,
their heads in cloud, their feet in moving patches
of scuffed-up white.
Glass chimneys, flexible, attenuated,
sacerdotal beings of glass . . . I watched
the water spiral up in them like smoke.
Beautiful, yes, but not much company.

I often gave way to self-pity.
"Do I deserve this? I suppose I must.
I wouldn't be here otherwise. Was there
a moment when I actually chose this?
I don't remember, but there could have been."
What's wrong about self-pity, anyway?
With my legs dangling down familiarly
over a crater's edge, I told myself
"Pity should begin at home." So the more
pity I felt, the more I felt at home.

The sun set in the sea; the same odd sun
rose from the sea,
and there was one of it and one of me.
The island had one kind of everything:
one tree snail, a bright violet-blue
with a thin shell, crept over everything,
over the one variety of tree,
a sooty, scrub affair.
Snail shells lay under these in drifts
and, at a distance,
you'd swear that they were beds of irises.
There was one kind of berry, a dark red.
I tried it, one by one, and hours apart.
Sub-acid, and not bad, no ill effects;
and so I made home-brew. I'd drink
the awful, fizzy stinging stuff
that went straight to my head
and play my home-made flute
(I think it had the weirdest scale on earth)
and, dizzy, whoop and dance among the goats.
Home-made, home-made! But aren't we all?
I felt a deep affection for
the smallest of my island industries.
No, not exactly, since the smallest was
a miserable philosophy.

Because I didn't know enough.
Why didn't I know enough of something?
Greek drama or astronomy? The books
I'd read were full of blanks;
the poems – well, I tried
reciting to my iris-beds,
"They flash upon that inward eye,
which is the bliss ... " The bliss of what?
One of the first things that I did
when I got back was look it up.

The island smelled of goat and guano.
The goats were white, so were the gulls,

[134]

and both too tame, or else they thought
I was a goat, too, or a gull.
*Baa, baa, baa* and *shriek, shriek, shriek,*
*baa* ... *shriek* ... *baa* ... I still can't shake
them from my ears; they're hurting now.
The questioning shrieks, the equivocal replies
over a ground of hissing rain
and hissing, ambulating turtles
got on my nerves.

When all the gulls flew up at once, they sounded
like a big tree in a strong wind, its leaves.
I'd shut my eyes and think about a tree,
an oak, say, with real shade, somewhere.
I'd heard of cattle getting island-sick.
I thought the goats were.
One billy-goat would stand on the volcano
I'd christened *Mont d'Espoir* or *Mount Despair*
(I'd time enough to play with names),
and bleat and bleat, and sniff the air.
I'd grab his beard and look at him.
His pupils, horizontal, narrowed up
and expressed nothing, or a little malice.
I got so tired of the very colors!
One day I dyed a baby goat bright red
with my red berries, just to see
something a little different.
And then his mother wouldn't recognize him.

Dreams were the worst. Of course I dreamed of food
and love, but they were pleasant rather
than otherwise. But then I'd dream of things
like slitting a baby's throat, mistaking it
for a baby goat. I'd have
nightmares of other islands
stretching away from mine, infinities
of islands, islands spawning islands,
like frogs' eggs turning into polliwogs

of islands, knowing that I had to live
on each and every one, eventually,
for ages, registering their flora,
their fauna, their geography.

Just when I thought I couldn't stand it
another minute longer, Friday came.
(Accounts of that have everything all wrong.)
Friday was nice.
Friday was nice, and we were friends.
If only he had been a woman!
I wanted to propagate my kind,
and so did he, I think, poor boy.
He'd pet the baby goats sometimes,
and race with them, or carry one around.
– Pretty to watch; he had a pretty body.

And then one day they came and took us off.

Now I live here, another island,
that doesn't seem like one, but who decides?
My blood was full of them; my brain
bred islands. But that archipelago
has petered out. I'm old.
I'm bored, too, drinking my real tea,
surrounded by uninteresting lumber.
The knife there on the shelf –
it reeked of meaning, like a crucifix.
It lived. How many years did I
beg it, implore it, not to break.
I knew each nick and scratch by heart,
the bluish blade, the broken tip,
the lines of wood-grain on the handle . . .
Now it won't look at me at all.
The living soul has dribbled away.
My eyes rest on it and pass on.

The local museum's asked me to
leave everything to them:

the flute, the knife, the shrivelled shoes,
my shedding goatskin trousers
(moths have got in the fur),
the parasol that took me such a time
remembering the way the ribs should go.
It still will work but, folded up,
looks like a plucked and skinny fowl.
How can anyone want such things?
– And Friday, my dear Friday, died of measles
seventeen years ago come March.

*to carry*
*curse –*
*to plague*
*a companion*

*At one*
*we'll grow*

# MURIEL RUKEYSER
## 1913–1981

## *George Robinson: Blues*

Gauley Bridge is a good town for Negroes, they let us stand
    around, they let us stand
around on the sidewalks if we're black or brown.
Vanetta's over the trestle, and that's our town.

The hill makes breathing slow, slow breathing after you row the
    river,
and the graveyard's on the hill, cold in the springtime blow,
and the graveyard's up on high, and the town is down below.

Did you ever bury thirty-five men in a place in back of your house,
thirty-five tunnel workers the doctors didn't attend,
died in the tunnel camps, under rocks, everywhere, world without
    end.

When a man said I feel poorly, for any reason, any weakness or
    such,
letting up when he couldn't keep going barely,
the Cap and company come and run him off the job surely.

I've put them
DOWN from the tunnel camps
to the graveyard on the hill,
tin-cans all about – it fixed them! –
TUNNELITIS
hold themselves up
at the side of a tree,
I can go right now
to that cemetery.

When the blast went off the boss would call out, Come, let's go
    back,
when that heavy loaded blast went white, Come let's go back,
telling us hurry, hurry, into the falling rocks and muck.

The water they would bring had dust in it, our drinking water,
the camps and their groves were colored with dust,
we cleaned our clothes in the groves, but we always had the dust.
Looked like somebody sprinkled flour all over the parks and groves,
it stayed and the rain couldn't wash it away and it twinkled
that white dust really looked pretty down around our ankles.

As dark as I am, when I came out at morning after the tunnel at
        night,
with a white man, nobody could have told which man was white.
The dust had covered us both, and the dust was white.

# GWENDOLYN BROOKS
## 1917–

## *"Negro" Hero*
### *to suggest Dorie Miller*

I had to kick their law into their teeth in order to save them.
However, I have heard that sometimes you have to deal
Devilishly with drowning men in order to swim them to shore.
Or they will haul themselves and you to the trash and the fish
      beneath.
(When I think of this, I do not worry about a few
Chipped teeth.)

It is good I gave glory, it is good I put gold on their name.
Or there would have been spikes in the afterward hands.
But let us speak only of my success and the pictures in the
      Caucasian dailies
As well as the Negro weeklies. For I am a gem.
(They are not concerned that it was hardly The Enemy my fight
      was against
But them.)

It was a tall time. And of course my blood was
Boiling about in my head and straining and howling and singing
      me on.
Of course I was rolled on wheels of my boy itch to get at the gun.
Of course all the delicate rehearsal shots of my childhood massed in
      mirage before me.
Of course I was child
And my first swallow of the liquor of battle bleeding black air dying
      and demon noise
Made me wild.

It was kinder than that, though, and I showed like a banner my
      kindness.
I loved. And a man will guard when he loves.
Their white-gowned democracy was my fair lady.

With her knife lying cold, straight, in the softness of her sweet-
    flowing sleeve.
But for the sake of the dear smiling mouth and the stuttered
    promise I toyed with my life.
I threw back! – I would not remember
Entirely the knife.

Still – am I good enough to die for them, is my blood bright
    enough to be spilled,
Was my constant back-question – are they clear
On this? Or do I intrude even now?
Am I clean enough to kill for them, do they wish me to kill
For them or is my place while death licks his lips and strides to
    them
In the galley still?

(In a southern city a white man said
Indeed, I'd rather be dead;
Indeed, I'd rather be shot in the head
Or ridden to waste on the back of a flood
Than saved by the drop of a black man's blood.)

Naturally, the important thing is, I helped to save them, them and a
    part of their democracy.
Even if I had to kick their law into their teeth in order to do that
    for them.
And I am feeling well and settled in myself because I believe it was
    a good job,
Despite the possible horror: that they might prefer the
Preservation of their law in all its sick dignity and their knives
To the continuation of their creed
And their lives.

# MAY SWENSON
## 1919–1989

## *First Walk on the Moon*

Ahead, the sun's face in a flaring hood,
was wearing the moon, a mask of shadow
that stood between. Cloudy earth
waned, gibbous, while our target grew:
an occult bloom, until it lay beneath
the fabricated insect we flew. Pitched
out of orbit we yawned in, to impact
softly on that circle.

                Not "ground"
the footpads found for traction.
So far, we haven't the name.
So call it "terrain," pitted and pocked
to the round horizon (which looked
too near): a slope of rubble where
protuberant cones, dish-shaped hollows,
great sockets glared, half blind
with shadow, and smaller sucked-in folds
squinted, like blowholes on a scape
of whales.

              Rigid and pneumatic, we
emerged, white twin uniforms on the dark
"mare," our heads transparent spheres,
the outer visors gold. The light was
glacier bright, our shadows long,
thin fissures, of "ink." We felt neither
hot nor cold.

             Our boot cleats sank
into "grit, something like glass,"
but sticky. Our tracks remain
on what was virgin "soil." But that's
not the name.

[142]

There was no air there,
no motion, no sound outside our heads.
We brought what we breathed
on our backs: the square papooses we
carried were our life sacks. We spoke
in numbers, fed the rat-a-tat-tat of data
to amplified earth. We saw no spoor
that any had stepped before us. Not
a thing has been born here, and nothing
has died, we thought.

We had practiced
to walk, but we toddled (with caution,
lest ambition make us fall
to our knees on that alien "floor").
We touched nothing with bare hands.
Our gauntlets lugged the cases of gear,
deployed our probes and emblems,
set them prudently near the insect liftoff
station, with its flimsy ladder to home.

All day it was night, the sky black
vacuum, though the strobe of the low sun
smote ferocious on that "loam."
We could not stoop, but scooped up
"clods" of the clinging "dust," that flowed
and glinted black, like "graphite."
So, floating while trotting, hoping not
to stub our toe, we chose and catalogued
unearthly "rocks." These we stowed.

And all night it was day, you could say,
with cloud-cuddled earth in the zenith,
a ghost moon that swiveled. The stars
were all displaced, or else were not
the ones we knew. Maneuvering by numbers
copied from head to head, we surveyed
our vacant outpost. Was it a "petrified
sea bed," inert "volcanic desert," or
crust over quivering "magma," that might
quake?

It was possible to stand there.
And we planted a cloth "flower":
our country colors we rigged to blow
in the non-wind. We could not lift
our arms eye-high (they might deflate)
but our camera was a pistol, the trigger
built into the grip, and we took each
other's pictures, shooting from the hip.
Then bounced and loped euphoric,
enjoying our small weight.

                    Our flash
eclipsed the sun at takeoff. We left our
insect belly "grounded," and levitated,
standing in its head. The dark dents
of our boots, unable to erode, mark how
we came: two white mechanic knights,
the first, to make tracks of some kind
of "sand." The footpads found it solid, so
we "landed." But that's not the right name.

*Note*: The men of Apollo 11, arriving in their landing module, Eagle, were the
first to put tracks on the moon, 1969.

## MONA VAN DUYN
### 1921–

# *The Gardener to His God*

*"Amazing research proves simple prayer makes flowers grow many
times faster, stronger, larger."*
                    Advertisement in the *Flower Grower*

I pray that the great world's flowering stay as it is,
that larkspur and snapdragon keep to their ordinary size,
and bleedingheart hang in its old way, and Judas tree
stand well below oak, and old oaks color the fall sky.
For the myrtle to keep underfoot, and no rose
to send up a swollen face, I pray simply.

There is no disorder but the heart's. But if love goes leaking
outward, if shrubs take up its monstrous stalking,
all greenery is spurred, the snapping lips are overgrown,
and over oaks red hearts hang like the sun.
Deliver us from its giant gardening, from walking
all over the earth with no rest from its disproportion.

Let all flowers turn to stone before ever they begin to share
love's spaciousness, and faster, stronger, larger
grow from a sweet thought, before any daisy
turns, under love's gibberellic wish, to the day's eye.
Let all blooms take shape from cold laws, down from a cold air
let come their small grace or measurable majesty.

For in every place but love the imagination lies
in its limits. Even poems draw back from images
of that one country, on top of whose lunatic stemming
whoever find himself there must sway and cling
until the high cold God takes pity, and it all dies
down, down into the great world's flowering.

# JOHN ASHBERY
## 1927–

## *On The Empress's Mind*

Let's make a bureaucracy.
First, we can have long lists of old things,
and new things repackaged as old ones.
We can have turrets, a guiding wall.
Soon the whole country will come to look over it.

Let us, by all means, have things in night light:
partly visible. The rudeness that poetry often brings
after decades of silence will help. Many
will be called to account. This means that laundries
in their age-old way will go on foundering. Is it any help
that motorbikes whiz up, to ask for directions
or colored jewelry, so that one can go about one's visit
a tad less troubled than before, lightly composed?

No one knows what it's about anymore.
Even in the beginning one had grave misgivings
but the enthusiasm of departure swept them away
in the green molestation of spring.

We were given false information on which
our lives were built, a pier
extending far out into a swollen river.
Now, even these straws are gone.

Tonight the party will be better than ever.
So many mystery guests. And the rain that sifts
through sobbing trees, that excited skiff . . .
Others have come and gone and wrought no damage.
Others have caught, or caused darkness, a long vent
in the original catastrophe no one has seen.
They have argued. Tonight will be different. Is it better for you?

# ANNE SEXTON
## 1928–1974

## *Jesus Dies*

From up here in the crow's nest
I see a small crowd gather.
Why do you gather, my townsmen?
There is no news here.
I am not a trapeze artist.
I am busy with My dying.
Three heads lolling,
bobbing like bladders.
No news.
The soldiers down below
laughing as soldiers have done for centuries.
No news.
We are the same men,
you and I,
the same sort of nostrils,
the same sort of feet.
My bones are oiled with blood
and so are yours.
My heart pumps like a jack rabbit in a trap
and so does yours.
I want to kiss God on His nose and watch Him sneeze
and so do you.
Not out of disrespect.
Out of pique.
Out of a man-to-man thing.
I want heaven to descend and sit on My dinner plate
and so do you.
I want God to put His steaming arms around Me
and so do you.
Because we need.
Because we are sore creatures.
My townsmen,
go home now.

I will do nothing extraordinary.
I will not divide in two.
I will not pick out My white eyes.
Go now,
this is a personal matter,
a private affair and God knows
none of your business.

# RICHARD HOWARD
## 1929–

# *1915: A Pre-Raphaelite Ending,*
# *London*

### *for Sanford Friedman*

Save it all; you do not know
the value things will come to have until
the world grows dim around you, and your things
– however doubtful in the changing light,
      things are what you have
      left. And all you have.
Once the Zeppelins are gone
– and I shall be gone too, then, surely gone
out of this chair, this bed, this *furniture*,
there will be time enough to throw away
      whatever is left.
      Keep the papers here
    in these boxes where I have
kept them so long to myself – for myself,
till the Zeppelins. I am not certain
(how could I be, kept here out of harm's way)
      what Zeppelins *are*.
      You would not expect
    the daughter of an Oxford
livery-stable keeper to know it . . .
Your father was not fond of animals.
He said once he might get to like a horse,
      if he had the time.
      Take care with the ones
    on top, they are photographs.
Read out what is scrawled there: "Dearest Janey,
Dodgson will be here tomorrow at noon,
do come as early as you can manage."
      They have no backing
      and break like dead leaves.

Often Gabriel painted
from these when he could not see me. He said
Mr. Dodgson knew what to leave out. Give
that one to me. No, it does not matter.
            I want to hear you
            say the words aloud:
"Absence can never make me
so far from you again as your presence did
for years. Yet no one seems alive now –
the places empty of you are empty
            of all life." Of course
            William knew of it,
    but trusted. He had a deep
understanding of one side of life, and
invented the other. Remember how
he loved to list the things he owned,
            grade and tabulate . . .
            Why, he could not sit
    in this room without an arm
about my waist – when others were by. Then
one time he burst out in a rage: "Is it
nothing but make-believe, am I no more
            than Louis XVI
            tinkering with locks?"
    You know what his rages were –
I saw him drive his head against that wall,
making a dent in the plaster. "With locks,"
he said, "tinkering with locks, and too late . . ."
            With locks, did he say,
            or clocks? Clocks, I think.
    How can a woman resolve
her marriage, save by lies? I have not learned
from others. I speak of my own life. She
stays at home, the man goes forth. A husband's
            absence, a daughter's
            anger, a lover's
    suspicion – that is her lot.
What survives is the resistance we bring
to life, the courage of our features, not

the strain life brings to us. Each doctor says
        a different thing
        when I awaken
    gasping in the night. How well
one has to be, to be ill! *Tragic health*,
Mr. Ruskin called it. That is his hand,
I recognize the stroke. He gave me this
        during a long walk
        after Gabriel
    was cold in his grave, at last.
No one may see them till after my death,
and you must wait for that. William waited,
but I have not died. He came to Kelmscott
        – the meadows flooded
        that year, and the noise
    of water filled the air. "Jane,
I wegwet," he said – he could not pronounce
his r's, odd in a man named Ruskin. Then
a tortoise-shell butterfly settled on
        my shoulder, but he
        refused to notice.
    "I cannot admire any
lower in the scale than a fish," he said,
"I have the best disposition toward slugs
and gnats, but why they exist I do not
        understand." He stopped,
        though, to pick some cress
    growing by the path – and what
he regretted was that he could not bear
to destroy these drawings he would give me
on the condition that I never look
        at them in my life.
        They must be naked
    drawings of me, beautiful
indeed if Mr. Ruskin could not burn
what he bought to keep the world and William
from seeing. There are his words on the seal:
        "I should as soon try
        finding fault with him

as with a nightshade-blossom
or a thundercloud. Of him and of these
all I can say is that God made him, and
*they* are greatly made. To me they may be
        dreadful or deadly.
        There is certainly
    something wrong with him – awful
in proportion to the power it affects
and renders at present useless. So it was
with Turner, so with Byron." With this came
        a great quantity
        of ivory-dust
    to be made into a jelly,
which it seems is an excellent physic
for invalids. Not even William failed
to guess the shame beneath the show –
        he had the habit,
        months and years after,
    of taking up the packet
and regarding its black seal with the eye
of an enemy. I was like Mariana
in the moated grange, listening too often
        to the mouse shrieking
        in the wainscot. "I
    can't paint you but I love you –"
he said that when I sat to them, at Oxford.
He first saw me there, and his destiny
was defined ... Gabriel called him a name:
        Tops, the poetic
        upholstery-man.
    Their mothers all outlived them –
Gabriel, William, *and* Mr. Ruskin.
It was an abyss then, an imbroglio
then and after. The reciprocal
        life of "well persons"
        grew impossible.
    Moments come when the pattern
is laid before us, plain. And then we know
the limitations, accidentally

repeated, are the stuff of life. They will
      return again, for
      they are just . . . ourselves.
    Then we know that this and none
other will be our life. And so begins
a long decay – we die from day to dream,
and common speech we answer with a scream.
        Put those things aside.
        Here are the letters
     from Iceland, times were mended
for us both, by then. William was away
from the loud group of yellowing rowdies
who called themselves "communists" – and from me.
        And he wrote, always,
        lovely letters – if
    you did not have to hear him
say the words, as if he were breaking off
bones, throwing them aside – it was, through him,
an ancient voice speaking, or a voice from
        a previous life
        jerking the words out
    of a body which it had
nothing to do with. Take one from the lot,
they are all the same, though like no one else:
freeing ourselves we forge our own chains.
        "I lie often out
        on the cliffs, lazy
    themselves, all grown with gold broom,
not athletic as at Dover, not gaunt
as at Shields, and through the mist of summer
sea and sky are one, while just underfoot
        the boats, together,
        stand immovable –
    as if their shadows clogged them.
So one may lie and symbolize until
one falls asleep, and that be a symbol
as well." Take the last one. I remember
        the last words the best.
        "As for living, dear,

  people like those you speak of
don't know what life means or death either, save
for one or two moments when something breaks
the crust, and they act for the time as if
    they were sensitive."
   William's mind was set
  on things more significant
than human lives, individual lives . . .
During the last illness, Dolmetsch came here
to play Byrd to him on the virginals.
    He broke into tears
    – of joy, only joy,
  at the opening phrases
of a pavane. Then he saw white bodies
moving, crowned and bound with gold. That faded.
I went for the post, and when I returned
    he stifled the blood
    streaming from his mouth
  and held fast to my gown, one
of his designs I had worn all those days.
"The clothes are well enough," were his last words,
"but where has the body gone?" Is there more
    besides, in the box?
    I thought no. Will you
  do as I say, save it all –
the rest of the things are mere images,
not medieval – only middle-aged:
lifelike but lifeless, wonderful but dead.
    These are mine. Save them.
    I have nothing save them.

# ADRIENNE RICH
## 1929–

## *The Loser*

1.

I kissed you, bride and lost, and went
home from that bourgeois sacrament,
your cheek still tasting cold upon
my lips that gave you benison
with all the swagger that they knew –
as losers somehow learn to do.

Your wedding made my eyes ache; soon
the world would be worse off for one
more golden apple dropped to the ground
without the least protesting sound,
and you would windfall lie, and we
forget your shimmer on the tree.

Beauty is always wasted; if
not Mignon's song sung to the deaf,
at all events to the unmoved.
A face like yours cannot be loved
long or seriously enough.
Almost, we seem to hold it off.


2.

Well, you are tougher than I thought.
Now when the wash with ice hangs taut
this morning of St. Valentine,
I see you strip the squeaking line,
your body weighed against the load,
and all my groans can do no good.

Because you still are beautiful,
Though squared and stiffened by the pull
of what nine windy years have done.
You have three daughters, lost a son.

[155]

I see all your intelligence
flung into that unwearied stance.

My envy is of no avail.
I turn my head and wish him well
who chafed your beauty into use
and lives forever in a house
lit by the friction of your mind.
You stagger in against the wind.

# TED HUGHES
## 1930–

## *Cleopatra to the Asp*

The bright mirror I braved: the devil in it
Loved me like my soul, my soul:
Now that I seek myself in a serpent
My smile is fatal.

Nile moves in me; my thighs splay
Into the squalled Mediterranean;
My brain hides in that Abyssinia
Lost armies foundered toward.

Desert and river unwrinkle again.
Seeming to bring them the waters that make drunk
Caesar, Pompey, Antony I drank.
Now let the snake reign.

A half-deity out of Capricorn,
This rigid Augustus mounts
With his sword virginal indeed; and has shorn
Summarily the moon-horned river

From my bed. May the moon
Ruin him with virginity! Drink me, now, whole
With coiled Egypt's past; then from my delta
Swim like a fish toward Rome.

# LUCILLE CLIFTON
## 1936-

### *powell*
### *(officer charged with the beating*
### *of rodney king)*

this is that dream i wake from
crying, then clutch my sleeping wife
and rock her until i fall again
onto a battlefield. there,
they surround me, nations of darkness
speaking a language i do not understand
and i suspect that something about my life
they know and hate and i hate them
for knowing it so well. my son,
i think about my son, my golden daughter,
and as they surround me, nearer, nearer,
i reach to pick up anything,
a tool, a stick, a weapon and
something begins to die. this
is that dream.

## ALICIA OSTRIKER
## 1937–

# *A Minor Van Gogh (He Speaks):*

The strokes are pulses: from my shapely cloud
And sky descending to distant hills
And closer hills, there is a far white tower
That rests, and in the foreground a muddy earth
Of ochre and purple strips, here is my soft clay, my
Bushy juicy green in the corner
And my plowman whom I make at
Dawn forever following his horse
Down the middle of the world. The strokes
Rush forward, waving their hats, identical,
All elements alike, all particles
Of Christ's material dancing, even
The shadowed furrow saying *I exist, I live*!
I also live, and make this form of Christ,
Locked in the light of earth, compassionate.
                    *"Landscape with Plowman," Fogg Museum*

# FRANK BIDART
## 1939–

## *Ellen West*

I love sweets, –
             heaven
would be dying on a bed of vanilla ice cream . . .

But my true self
is thin, all profile

and effortless gestures, the sort of blond
elegant girl whose
                    body is the image of her soul.

– My doctors tell me I must give up
this ideal;
        but I
WILL NOT . . . cannot.

Only to my husband I'm not simply a "case."

But he is a fool. He married
meat, and thought it was a wife.

●  ●  ●

Why am I a girl?

I ask my doctors, and they tell me they
don't know, that it is just "given."

But it has such
implications – ;
                and sometimes,
I even feel like a girl.

• • •

Now, at the beginning of Ellen's thirty-second year, her physical condition has deteriorated still further. Her use of laxatives increases beyond measure. Every evening she takes sixty to seventy tablets of a laxative, with the result that she suffers tortured vomiting at night and violent diarrhea by day, often accompanied by a weakness of the heart. She has thinned down to a skeleton, and weighs only 92 pounds.

• • •

About five years ago, I was in a restaurant,
eating alone
            with a book. I was
not married, and often did that . . .

– I'd turn down
dinner invitations, so I could eat alone;

I'd allow myself two pieces of bread, with
butter, at the beginning, and three scoops of
vanilla ice cream, at the end, –

                              sitting there alone
with a book, both in the book
and out of it, waited on, idly
watching people, –

                  when an attractive young man
and woman, both elegantly dressed,
sat next to me.
            She was beautiful – ;

with sharp, clear features, a good
bone structure – ;
                  if she took her make-up off
in front of you, rubbing cold cream
again and again across her skin, she still would be

beautiful –
        more beautiful.

And he, –
        I couldn't remember when I had seen a man
so attractive. I didn't know why. He was almost

a male version
        of her, –

I had the sudden, mad notion that I
wanted to be his lover . . .

– Were they married?
                were *they* lovers?

They didn't wear wedding rings.

Their behavior was circumspect. They discussed
politics. They didn't touch . . .

– How could I discover?

                Then, when the first course
arrived, I noticed the way

each held his fork out for the other

to taste what he had ordered . . .

                They did this
again and again, with pleased looks, indulgent
smiles, for each course,
                more than once for *each* dish – ;
much too much for just friends . . .

– Their behavior somehow sickened me;

the way each *gladly*

put the *food* the other had offered *into his mouth* – ;

I knew what they were. I knew they slept together.

An immense depression came over me . . .

– I knew I could never
with such ease allow another to put food into my mouth:

happily *myself* put food into another's mouth – ;

I knew that to become a wife I would have to give up my ideal.

•　•　•

Even as a child,
I saw that the "natural" process of aging

is for one's middle to thicken –
one's skin to blotch;

as happened to my mother.
And her mother.
                    *I loathed "Nature."*

At twelve, pancakes
became the most terrible thought there is . . .

I shall *defeat* "Nature."

In the hospital, when they
weigh me, I wear weights secretly sewn into my belt.

•　•　•

January 16. The patient is allowed to eat in her room, but comes
readily with her husband to afternoon coffee. Previously she had stoutly
resisted this on the ground that she did not really eat but devoured
like a wild animal. This she demonstrated with utmost realism . . . Her

physical examination showed nothing striking. Salivary glands are markedly enlarged on both sides.

   January 21. Has been reading *Faust* again. In her diary, writes that art is the "mutual permeation" of the "world of the body" and the "world of the spirit." Says that her own poems are "hospital poems ... weak – without skill or perseverance; only managing to beat their wings softly."

   February 8. Agitation, quickly subsided again. Has attached herself to an elegant, very thin female patient. Homo-erotic component strikingly evident.

   February 15. Vexation, and torment. Says that her mind forces her always to think of eating. Feels herself degraded by this. Has entirely, for the first time in years, stopped writing poetry.

•  •  •

Callas is my favorite singer, but I've only
seen her once – ;

I've never forgotten that night ...

– It was in *Tosca*, she had long before
lost weight, her voice
had been, for years,
                    deteriorating, half itself ...

When her career began, of course, she was fat,

enormous – ; in the early photographs,
sometimes I almost don't recognize her ...

The voice too then was enormous –

healthy; robust; subtle; but capable of
crude effects, even vulgar,
                    almost out of
high spirits, too much health ...

[164]

But soon she felt that she must lose weight, –
that all she was trying to express

was obliterated by her body,
buried in flesh – ;
               abruptly, within
four months, she lost at least sixty pounds . . .

– The gossip in Milan was that Callas
had swallowed a tapeworm.

But of course she hadn't.

              The *tapeworm*
was her *soul* . . .

– How her soul, uncompromising,
insatiable,
           must have loved eating the flesh from her bones,

revealing this extraordinarily
mercurial; fragile; masterly creature . . .

– But irresistibly, nothing
*stopped* there; the huge voice

also began to change: at first, it simply diminished
in volume, in size,
              then the top notes became
shrill, unreliable – at last,
usually not there at all . . .

– No one knows *why*. Perhaps her mind,
ravenous, still insatiable, sensed

that to struggle with the *shreds* of a voice

must make her artistry subtler, more refined,
more capable of expressing humiliation,
rage, betrayal . . .

– Perhaps the opposite. Perhaps her spirit
loathed the unending struggle

to *embody* itself, to *manifest* itself, on a stage whose

mechanics, and suffocating customs,
seemed expressly designed to annihilate spirit . . .

– I know that in *Tosca*, in the second act,
when, humiliated, hounded by Scarpia,
she sang *Vissi d'arte*
                   – "I lived for art" –

and in torment, bewilderment, at the end she asks,
with a voice reaching
                 harrowingly for the notes,

"Art has *repaid* me LIKE THIS?"

                           I felt I was watching
autobiography –
             an art; skill;
virtuosity

miles distant from the usual soprano's
athleticism, –
             the usual musician's dream
of virtuosity *without* content . . .

– I wonder what she feels, now,
listening to her recordings.

For they have already, within a few years,
begun to date . . .

Whatever they express
they express through the style of a decade
and a half – ;
             a style *she* helped create . . .

– She must know that now
she probably would *not* do a trill in
*exactly* that way, –
     that the whole sound, atmosphere,
*dramaturgy* of her recordings

have just slightly become those of the past . . .

– Is it bitter? Does her soul
tell her

that she was an *idiot* ever to think
anything
    *material* wholly could satisfy? . . .

– Perhaps it says: *The only way*
*to escape*
*the History of Styles*

*is not to have a body.*

●   ●   ●

When I open my eyes in the morning, my great
mystery
    stands before me . . .

– I *know* that I am intelligent; therefore

the inability not to fear food
day-and-night; this unending hunger
ten minutes after I have eaten . . .
       a childish
dread of eating; hunger which can have no cause, –

half my mind says that all this
is *demeaning* . . .

    Bread
for days on end

drives all real thought from my brain . . .

– Then I think, No. The ideal of being thin

conceals the ideal
*not* to have a body – ;
               which is NOT trivial . . .

This wish seems now as much a "given" of my existence

as the intolerable
fact that I am dark-complexioned; big-boned;
and once weighed
one hundred and sixty-five pounds . . .

– But then I think, *No*. That's too simple, –

without a body, who can
*know* himself at all?
             Only by
acting; choosing; rejecting; have I
made myself –
           discovered who and what *Ellen* can be . . .

– But then again I think, NO. This *I* is anterior

to name; gender; action;
fashion;
        MATTER ITSELF, –

. . . trying to stop my hunger with FOOD
is like trying to appease thirst
             with ink.

            ● ● ●

March 20. Result of the consultation: Both gentlemen agree completely with my prognosis and doubt any therapeutic usefulness of commitment even more emphatically than I. All three of us are agreed

that it is not a case of obsessional neurosis and not one of manic-
depressive psychosis, and that no definitely reliable therapy is possible.
We therefore resolved to give in to the patient's demand for discharge.

• • •

The train-ride yesterday
was far *worse* than I expected . . .

                        In our compartment
were ordinary people: a student;
a woman; her child; –

they had ordinary bodies, pleasant faces;
                        but I thought
I was surrounded by creatures

with the pathetic, desperate
desire to be *not* what they were: –

the student was short,
and carried his body as if forcing
it to be taller – ;

the woman showed her gums when she smiled,
and often held her
hand up to hide them – ;

the child
seemed to cry simply because it was
small; a dwarf, and helpless . . .

– I was hungry. I had insisted that my husband
*not* bring food . . .

After about thirty minutes, the woman
peeled an orange

to quiet the child. She put a section
into its mouth – ;

              immediately it spit it out.

The piece fell to the floor.

– She pushed it with her foot through the dirt
toward me
several inches.

My husband saw me staring
down at the piece . . .

– I didn't move; how I wanted
to reach out,

             and as if invisible

shove it in my mouth – ;

my body
became rigid. As I stared at him,
I could see him staring

at me, –

          then he looked at the student – ; at the woman – ; then
back to me . . .

I didn't move.

– At last, he bent down, and
casually

          threw it out the window.

He looked away.

– I got up to leave the compartment, then
saw his face, –

his eyes
were red;

      and I saw

– *I'm sure I saw* –

disappointment.

             • • •

On the third day of being home she is as if transformed. At breakfast she eats butter and sugar, at noon she eats so much that – for the first time in thirteen years! – she is satisfied by her food and gets really full. At afternoon coffee she eats chocolate creams and Easter eggs. She takes a walk with her husband, reads poems, listens to recordings, is in a positively festive mood, and all heaviness seems to have fallen away from her. She writes letters, the last one a letter to the fellow patient here to whom she had become so attached. In the evening she takes a lethal dose of poison, and on the following morning she is dead. "She looked as she had never looked in life – calm and happy and peaceful."

             • • •

Dearest. – I remember how
at eighteen,

      on hikes with friends, when
they rested, sitting down to joke or talk,

I circled
around them, afraid to hike ahead alone,

yet afraid to rest
when I was not yet truly thin.

You and, yes, my husband, –
you and he

have by degrees drawn me within the circle;
forced me to sit down at last on the ground.

I am grateful.

But something in me *refuses* it.

– How eager I have been
to compromise, to kill this *refuser*, –

but each compromise, each attempt
to poison an ideal
which often seemed to *me* sterile and unreal,

heightens my hunger.

I am crippled. I disappoint you.

Will you greet with anger, or
happiness,

the news which might well reach you
before this letter?

Your *Ellen*.

# SEAMUS HEANEY
## 1939–

## *Bog Queen*

I lay waiting
between turf-face and demesne wall,
between heathery levels
and glass-toothed stone.

My body was braille
for the creeping influences:
dawn suns groped over my head
and cooled at my feet,

through my fabrics and skins
the seeps of winter
digested me,
the illiterate roots

pondered and died
in the cravings
of stomach and socket.
I lay waiting

on the gravel bottom,
my brain darkening,
a jar of spawn
fermenting underground

dreams of Baltic amber.
Bruised berries under my nails,
the vital hoard reducing
in the crock of the pelvis.

My diadem grew carious,
gemstones dropped
in the peat floe
like the bearings of history.

My sash was a black glacier
wrinkling, dyed weaves
and phoenician stitchwork
retted on my breasts'

soft moraines.
I knew winter cold
like the nuzzle of fjords
at my thighs –

the soaked fledge, the heavy
swaddle of hides.
My skull hibernated
in the wet nest of my hair.

Which they robbed.
I was barbered
and stripped
by a turfcutter's spade

who veiled me again
and packed coomb softly
between the stone jambs
at my head and my feet.

Till a peer's wife bribed him.
The plait of my hair,
a slimy birth-cord
of bog, had been cut

and I rose from the dark,
hacked bone, skull-ware,
frayed stitches, tufts,
small gleams on the bank.

# MICHAEL LONGLEY
## 1939–

## *Sulpicia*

Round this particular date I have drawn a circle
For Mars, dressed myself up for him, dressed to kill:
When I let my hair down I am a sheaf of wheat
And I bring in the harvest without cutting it.

Were he to hover above me like a bird of prey
I would lay my body out, his little country,
Fields smelling of flowers, flowers in the hedgerow –
And then I would put on an overcoat of snow.

I will stumble behind him through the undergrowth
Tracking his white legs, drawing about us both
The hunters' circle: among twisted nets and snares

I will seduce him, tangle his hairs with my hairs
While the stag dashes off on one of its tangents
And boars root safely along our circumference.

# SUNITI NAMJOSHI
## 1941–

## *Caliban's Journal*

He has chopped wood (very badly too) and carried logs for one whole day. I have done it for 12 years. She pities him. When I tried to show her my own hands, she would not look.

They are playing chess. I could learn too. I am not stupid. But they say it's a game intended for two. They have left me out.

These berries are nice, those are not nice. This water is fresh. That water is salt. I learnt. I learnt all that all by myself, and I told it to them. They were so pleased. But one day when I said to myself, "Miranda is nice," and told it to her, she didn't like it. She told it to him. I was whipped afterwards.

M thinks that the new men are very like gods. What is a god? I think M is a god. When I told it to her, she said I was stupid.

Today I made friends with the new gods. They were quite friendly. One of them asked me if I would like to be a god. I said, "Yes." So they gave me a potion. We all drank it. I remember laughing. They said I would make a splendid god. I wanted to tell M that now I was a god, but I fell asleep.

P says I must try to be good. I said that I would try to try. I looked at M, she didn't say anything.

Some of the "gods" want to take me with them. But I no longer believe that they are gods. I don't trust them.

If they all go away, I'll be left alone. That might be nice. But I might be lonely. I shall keep a journal. Soon, very soon, I shall people this island (with nice people).

# MICHAEL HEFFERNAN
## 1942–

## *The Message*

My husband had a knack of knowing things.
I don't know how he knew about Jack and me,
unless he had me tailed. I think he did,
though he would never say. All I know is
one day the Company security
came by my office and told me to leave,
clean out my desk and head for the parking lot.
Something about some Title 7 thing
about sexual harassment on the job
and use of corporate funds for personal business,
something about me and Jack that they found out
and wouldn't tell me how, and wouldn't tell me
which of us was the one that used the other.
I knew it was me, of course, and found out later
Jack had been reprimanded, but I was fired.
It had to be my husband. I didn't think
the crazy bastard knew me well enough,
he was so stupidly in love with me,
so painfully adoring. He'd call me up
whenever I was out of town and talk
about how he wished I'd taken him along,
and there I'd be with Jack or someone else
reaching his hands around me from behind
and trying to get inside me with his fingers.
One time I almost had to cry out loud.
My husband kept on talking and never noticed.
Finally I told him he didn't get the message.
This was in Dallas at Loews Anatole.
Jack had a towel on, I was in my robe.
My husband almost cried he was so sick,
so frustrated, I almost told him then,
but didn't want to yet. There was no reason
to let him know what he should figure out.

I had a plan to meet Jack in Shreveport.
I called him up at work at the chicken plant
down in Seguin – on the 800 line
so it wouldn't show up on the long-distance bill.
He ran the loading dock. He got his boss
to let him drive to pick me up in Shreveport
and take me to the plant, supposedly
on business. We both loved that part of it.
He turned his mileage in to the Company.
"We're really pulling a fast one," I told him –
"Why don't I sit and cross my legs and smile
and say to Randy, 'Thanks for letting Jack
come get me.'" Jack said no to that. Jack said
Randy was not the type to be amused.
"He'd kill me and care," Jack said. His sense of fun
stopped short where business and his job came in.
I understood, but that was not the point.
I told him I'd have new pink panties on,
maybe a new nightgown he could take off.
He said I wouldn't need one – I would spend
the whole time naked once I hit the door.
I said I'd work out doing deep knee bends
to get my thighs in shape for the plunges
and eat nothing but vegetables till then.
He promised he was only drinking tea
to get rid of his beergut. Exercise
was out for now. He had an injury
from playing softball and it hadn't healed.
He talked about his problems with Randy Wade
and how he needed to get out of there.
"I'll put my whole life in your hands," he said,
trying to make me sick with loving me.
I knew he wanted something, like they all did,
just like my husband always did. The fool
was so in love with me he never noticed
how much I had despised him all along.
All men are fools in love, without exception.
It turns them into boys, or animals.
They never notice where the line is drawn
between the thing they want and what I'll give them.

Sometimes I'd take the trophy off the shelf,
the one I won when I was three years old
for being the prettiest little girl in town,
and I would rub it till a piece of it
got smooth enough to show my face, almost
the way it looked in 1956,
and I could tell something of what they saw,
a tiny part of what I must have been
and could have gone on being, had I known
when I was young and stupid what would happen
and what I stood to lose when I got older.
The things a man demands, the things a woman
gives to a man that can't be taken back.
I tried to tell them, but they wouldn't hear me.
My husband wasn't any different.
He'd come to bed when I was half asleep
and bring one hand up under my nightgown
to spread his fingers nipple to nipple.
Before I could hold back, the other hand
was opening my thighs and slipping in,
and off would come the nightgown, then his mouth
stopped me from even thinking to say no,
and he had made me his the umpteenth time,
convinced I loved him for the afterthought
that always came when he would say he loved me
so I would say the same when he was done.
He'd lie there with his elbow on my hip,
and kiss my shoulders, breathe into my hair,
or sniff my armpit, which he said smelled good.
Sometimes he'd rub his hand along my face
like a blind man trying to learn the way I looked.
I'd close my eyes and wait for him to stop.
Slowly his hand grew lighter and the dark
would swallow up his fingers and my face
quit throbbing. He would say goodnight,
then lift himself away and roll aside.
We'd drop off by ourselves and sleep alone.
He must have seen our life continuing,
till one of us put the other in the ground.

Most likely it would be me that would bury him
and what would I have left but my own grave
and no one home to put me into it.

Jack said he liked the pillows in Pine Bluff
better than Little Rock or Russellville.
In Pine Bluff we had two adjoining rooms
with four beds, so the pillows came to eight
which put me high up like a harem girl
with my head back while he did what he did
down there, the way I liked it, till I came
and came and came and grabbed him by his hair
to come inside me while I kept on coming
till I lost count and we were soaking wet.
He'd rub his moustache in my pubic hair
like a soft brush until I'd start to tingle
and itch a little while he tongued my button.
In Shreveport we went windowshopping first.
I knew he hated that. I hoped he would.
I wanted him to hate something at least
so I could have him like I wanted him.
He wanted me for more reasons than one.
Two weeks before, he asked me a favor.
"You've got this inside track," he said. "Isn't it time
you did something for me?" My stomach turned
when he said that. I said I couldn't ask
too many favors. People would get suspicious,
and that would be the end of what they'd give me.
I saw him fingering his coffee cup
and tapping a pencil on the desk and thinking
"What can I get from her?" I stopped him dead.
I gave him my coldest major-player voice
and shut him up right there. "I'll put my whole
body in your hands," he said, after a pause.
"That's better," I said, in my sex-kitten voice.
He said he'd let me go – just for a while,
and couldn't wait to get me in Shreveport.
"Now, smile," he said, as if he had to know.
"I am," I said, and saw him sitting there

like a boy kicking his feet back and forth,
holding onto the porch-swing with both hands
and staring up the street for the ice-cream man.
There isn't one of them that can get past
the need for something sweet to get their tongues in.

That night in Shreveport there was something else
I had to tell him. I had seen my doctor.
He'd given me an EIA test in the office
and medication for chlamydia,
which should have gotten rid of it in a week.
I wasn't about to let Jack know. Instead,
I told him he would have to use a condom
because I had some kind of strep infection
that we could keep on passing back and forth.
He slipped a three-pack in with cigarettes
at the Superette on our way back from dinner.
He seemed to understand, but he thought twice
about getting down there like he always did.
I couldn't stand to have him ask me that,
so I gave him my signal just to come inside
and made him think that that was what I wanted,
and then I acted like he made me crazy.
I crawled back up the bed until my head
hung over and he knelt there with his knees
under my ribs and pushed me with it hard
and kept on pushing like he couldn't stop
or wouldn't, like he wanted to make me beg
to stop him, or to get it over with.
I tried to pull on him to make him come.
I rubbed his balls. I rubbed his abdomen.
Nothing could stop him. He was like a man
whose body was an instrument of torture
with a piledriver at the end of it
and belts and pulleys pushing it forever.
He wouldn't stop, no matter what I did.
Finally I thought I would pass out.
My head hurt and my neck was about to break.
I heard his voice. He said he liked the way

I looked without a head. And then he laughed.
He kept on laughing. I could feel him stretch
and then he burst, but there was nothing warm,
no sweet juice filling me over the brim,
just the cold air and Jack a long way off,
receding into nowhere, and me halfway
onto the floor, swallowed up in the dark.
I noticed the sharp smell of carpet-cleaner.
And then a hand reached down to pull me up
and lay me down. Jack rolled back where he was
and went to sleep. I pulled the covers up
and let him sleep there naked, in the cold.

Next morning he was up before I was.
He waited for me out in the parking lot
and put me in the car without a word.
We hardly talked at all the whole way down.
He saw me to my room at the motel
and went home to his wife. He called me once
the next day on his way to pick me up
to drive me to the airport in San Antonio.
I didn't call him for a day or so.
By that time somebody had turned us in.
My husband had moved out, leaving me the kids.
I called his answering machine. I said,
"You are a crazy mean son of a bitch.
You always have been one and always will be."
He called me back when I was gone. He said:
"I hope you find another line of work
or another crazy mean son of a bitch
like me to give you everything you want."
I played that message once then ran it back
to tape it over. Then I shut the blinds
over the sliding door to kill the light.
Out in the yard the cat was coming home
and crying for his dinner. The heat came on.
The blower made the blinds move side to side.

# AI
## 1947–

## *The Good Shepherd:*
## *Atlanta, 1981*

I lift the boy's body
from the trunk,
set it down,
then push it over the embankment
with my foot.
I watch it roll
down into the river
and feel I'm rolling with it,
feel the first cold slap of the water,
wheeze and fall down on one knee.
So tired, so cold.
Lord, I need a new coat,
not polyester, but wool,
new and pure
like the little lamb
I killed tonight.
With my right hand,
that same hand that hits
with such force,
I push myself up gently.
I know what I'd like –
some hot cocoa by the heater.

Once home, I stand at the kitchen sink,
letting the water run
till it overflows the pot,
then I remember the blood
in the bathroom
and so upstairs.
I take cleanser,
begin to scrub
the tub, tiles, the toilet bowl,

then the bathroom.
Mop, vacuum, and dust rag.
Work, work for the joy of it,
for the black boys
who know too much,
but not enough to stay away,
and sometimes a girl, the girls too.
How their hands
grab at my ankles, my knees.
And don't I lead them
like a good shepherd?
I stand at the sink,
where the water is still
overflowing the pot,
turn off the faucet,
then heat the water and sit down.
After the last sweet mouthful of chocolate
burns its way down my throat,
I open the library book,
the one on mythology,
and begin to read.
Saturn, it says, devours his children.
Yes, it's true, I know it.
An ordinary man, though, a man like me
eats and is full.
Only God is never satisfied.

# YUSEF KOMUNYAKAA
## 1947–

## *The Thorn Merchant's Mistress*

I was on my high
horse then. I
wore red with ease

& I knew how
to walk. There
were men undressing me

everywhere I went,
& women wishing
themselves in my place,

a swan unfractured
by August. I was still
a girl. If they

wanted culture,
I said Vivaldi
& Plato's Cave.

If they wanted
the streets, I said
Fuck you.

I knew how
to plead, Wait, Wait,
till I caught the eye

of some *deus ex
machina*. I was in
a deep dance

pulling the hidden
strings of nude
shadows. But when his car
drove by so slow
my heart caught

[185]

like a fat moth

in spider web. Goddamn!
I didn't know
how to say No.

# HEATHER McHUGH
## 1948–

## *Note Delivered by Female Impersonator*

Perversion interests me,
a three-legged dog in the driveway,
Coquilles Saint-Jacques
on plastic dishes,
anything up the ass.
All I ask is a little
retardation. Let me be more
imperative: walk your holy
three-dots-one-dash walk
but not so fast. Serve
and order, shove and retract,
dump and lap, drill
and withdraw, but
slowly. Slowly.
Let me be more specific:
you interest me.

# DAVID ST. JOHN
## 1949–

## *Quote Me Wrong Again and I'll Slit the Throat of Your Pet Iguana*

My Dear Editor Manchette:
I have been reading you with interest
These past few mornings, as I sit where I've
Always sat in the café at the edge of
The Champ-de-Mars, over coffee, absorbing the news
Of the world before taking up once again
My duties at the Ministry – the same café
You and I used to meet at when we were students,
Young lovers needing to get away from all
Of that eloquent rabble surrounding us . . .
Those days! Even then you wore
Those black wool suits you've become famous for,
Even then the peculiar *bolo* necktie you'd
Discovered on a trip to South America –
Your single affectation. Unless, of course, one
Wishes to count, now, the way you love
To stroll past all the banks
On the Champs-Élysées walking your pet iguana
On a thin leather leash dyed the most hideous
Scarlet. These are things one comes
Either to admire or to loathe in an old friend,
And in this case, I admit, I find your taste
As questionable as I find your politics,
Which are execrable, most especially offensive
Being your view of women as the necessary
Appendages one finds intruding upon a life,
Somewhat like doorknobs carved of Asian ivory.
Which leads me now to the issue of your
Recent editorials about the work of both my
Ministry and of my dear friend Madame Racine;
The fact you're without conscience
Is, of course, no news to me, nor that you'd turn

On anyone at all if it gave you the least
Morsel to write about – all of this I learned
Years ago. But it pains me to find that all
Of those nights you spent in my bed
With its lovely view of the Ile St-Louis from
The garret window of my student digs, even
The little logs of *chèvre* I brought to you
With the glass goblet of red wine,
The gifts I left – the white silk opera scarves
And the biographies of famous conservatives –
All of it meant nothing to you, I see now,
The way day after day in your articles
Or editorials you slander me or misquote me,
Using the text of my lecture at the Exposition
To make me appear ludicrous, crude, and of –
Let's be frank – an alternative sexual persuasion.
Of this last, let me say that certainly
I've found that I love women in a way I never
Loved you; there is such clarity of vision,
Of belief, of tenderness and desire that
No man can claim. Yet what gives you the right
To lie, to invent for *my* tongue the endless
Stupidities you print? Let me be clear, let me
Be forthright; let me point out for you
The way our own history has paralleled the history
Around us; let me draw for you a little portrait
Of the way things will never be for you again –
Your days are numbered, and with very few
Numbers indeed. Therefore, I'll say
This once in warning, so that
You can never claim that nothing passed
Between us, either then or now, so that I'll know
I've done my best to reconcile our pasts, even
The few pleasures those pasts together held –
And let me swear on the blood of my Mother
And Father and all of the Saints
That if you ever quote me wrong again, for any
Reason and in any context, I'll slit *quite elegantly*
The fat throat of your sickening pet iguana.

[189]

# RITA DOVE
## 1952–

## *Genie's Prayer*
## *Under the Kitchen Sink*

*Housebuilding was conceived a heroic effort to stop time, suspend decay and interrupt the ordained flow to ruin that started with Adam's fall.*

*from* House *by Tracy Kidder*

Hair and bacon grease, pearl button
popped in the search for a shawl, smashed radiant aluminum
foil, blunt shreds of wax paper –
nothing gets lost, you can't flush the shit
without it floating back in the rheumy eye of the bowl
or coagulating in the drop-belly of transitional pipes.
And who gets to drag his bad leg
into the kitchen and under the sink,
flashlight scattering roaches, rusted brillo pads
his earned divan?

        The hot water squeezed
to a trickle so she counted out the finger holes
and dialed her least-loved son.
I don't believe in stepping
in the goddamn shoes of any other man
but I came because I'm good at this, I'm good

with my hands; last March I bought some 2 by 4s
at Home Depot and honed them down
to the sleekest, blondest, free-standing bar
any mildewed basement in a cardboard housing tract
under the glass gloom of a factory clock
ever saw. I put the best bottles
behind it: Dimple scotch, crystal Gordon,
one mean nigger rye. I stacked the records.
Called two girls who like to perform on shag rugs,
spun my mirrored globe and watched.

They were sweet, like pet monkeys. I know
Mom called me over so I'd have to lurch up
the porch steps and she could click her tongue
and say, That's what you get for evil living. Christ,
she took in wash through fourteen children and
*he* left her every time, went off on a 9-month binge
while the ripening babies ate her rich thighs
to sticks.

                I was the last one; I'm Genie,
Eugene June Bug; the others made me
call them "Aunt" and "Uncle" in public.
All except Annalee – cancer screwed *her.*
She withered like my leg. She dragged her body
through the house like a favorite doll.

Yes, I'm a man born too late for
*Ain't-that-a-shame*, I'm a monkey
with a message and a heart like
my father who fell laughing to his knees
when it burst and 24 crows spilled
from his mouth and they were all named Jim.

When I'm finished here
I'm gonna build a breezeway next,
with real nice wicker on some astroturf.

# ARCHIE WELLER
## 1957–

## *Ngungalari*

I go. I go. I go.
I, Ngungalari,
last of the Kaneang tribe.
I leave my brown-skinned brothers
sitting like frogs by the river,
waiting for tomorrow's princess.
I leave my sisters with their ghosts
of the pale-eyed wadgula men.
Croaking like a crow I go,
shaking like a wind torn tree
and I not yet a woman.
Keep your Nellie Strongfellow
for Ngungalari is my name.
I am last and lost in this strange land
that once was mine.
I leave fathers with their hopes
and too-young mothers with their tears
and unborn children with their fears.
For like a chicken-hawk I soar
I fly
away
so free.
Cry not for me,
Ngungalari.
I leave you with your dreams.

# The Cross-Gendered
# Poem

To write in the voice of another means to speak for, through and of another's experience. This powerful act has long been the purview of the poet, whose dramatic and lyric monologues testify to the success of the imagination. To "cross gender" as well – that is, for a woman to write in the voice of a man, or a man in the voice of a woman – complicates the act, as conscious and unconscious issues are brought to bear on the persona and the poem. Here then is an anthology from a new perspective, a place where history, poetry, politics, psychology, sexuality and values collide.

The cross-gendered poem did not develop exclusively in response to a literary environment rife with sexism, nor to a monolithic and mostly male canon; poets have always written these poems. None the less, to read a cross-gendered poem requires consideration of the poem's historical moment, as well as the complex mores which both illuminate and darken that moment. It is of particular relevance to the history of the cross-gendered poem that the environment of sexism breeds both "self-censorship" and "silencing", as feminist theorists and critics have persuasively argued. As poet Frank Bidart has commented, the individual poet's "conscious and unconscious aesthetic refusals" also influence the composition of these works.[1]

This volume presents a new way of looking at a long-standing poetic phenomenon, a phenomenon of cross-gendered verse which, with few exceptions, remains largely unexplored by contemporary scholarship. Each of these cross-gendered monologues constructs a persona foreign and familiar to its author's experiences, regardless of the sexual orientation of the poet; as a result, how these poems explore gender issues proves integral to our understanding of these poems. Simply, we need to study these poems as gendered acts.

Certain ideas recur and change in the chronological arrangement of these poems. As such, these poetic constructions of gender, the body and sexuality may be shown to document historical trends. But poetry

[193]

has long served as a way of knowing, even if what is known contradicts the "facts" of the historical present. Thus these poems – while necessarily understood historically – should also be read out of and against history, and distinct from accepted notions of literary eras or "periods." These works have their own ways of being; the cross-gendered poem deserves its own history.

From the poet's perspective, the accommodations of the first-person monologue are many. Writing as another person or "Other" allows the poet to fictionalize and to speak freely, both; these poems offer the dramatic and lyric testimony of the imagination just as they explore personal concerns. This dual act of writing is made all the more challenging when gender is crossed, as the poem itself becomes a kind of performance – and, to borrow a term from Mikhail Bakhtin, gender becomes "ventriloquated." Historically, such performances have often perpetuated inequities – when, for example, women have been continually objectified and demeaned – but as this collection demonstrates, the cross-gendered poem has also been a haven for other, notable accomplishments in which the poet's empathy transcends sexism. It is important, too, that this volume presents many major poems by major poets, both female and male, for the complexity of the cross-gendered poem, experienced by the poet in terms of formal and psychological challenges, has long inspired greatness.

There may be a way to read this collection as a whole, to compile a list of recurrent icons or colloquialisms; to argue, as it were, a semiotics of cross-gendered poetry. In its accumulations of words, images and representations, such a reading would underscore the notion of how an individual's identity is constructed, how the self enacts itself culturally. But this reading should not exclude other ways of understanding the poems, since it admits little more than poetic fashion through the years – the metaphors and images which become convention – and the reader would be left with the sense, indeed, that clothes make the man. Rather wonderfully, these poems resist such singular readings because the cross-gendered poem is not merely a cross-dressed poem.

In current literary criticism, notions of a particular poem's relevance often seem relegated to an historical postscript, or to the primacy of presupposition, the sometimes indefensible premise on which an argument rests. In other words, we already assume that Wordsworth's "Michael" is a significant poem – why else would we be reading a book written about it? As a literary phenomenon outside the canon, the cross-gendered poem can air no such pretensions. The very nature of a work in which a woman writes in the voice of a man resonates socially and politically as well as poetically. Examining this social, political and poetic evidence remains the pleasure in careful study of the poems anthologized here. We wish to aid this study by opening avenues for discussion, raising recurrent and important themes. And, since we break new ground in introducing cross-gendered poems here, we begin by placing them alongside the most familiar form of "writing in voices," dramatic monologue.

## Dramatic monologue and the cross-gendered poem

When most of us think of first-person monologues in English, we think of the work of Browning or Tennyson. This is predictable because the Victorians emphasized and popularized the monologue form. We also have a general sense that a "dramatic monologue" must be any work with a first-person narrator, any "I" speaking the poem; how else, after all, are we to compare two poems as unlike as Robert Browning's "Porphyria's Lover" and Pope's "Eloisa to Abelard"? Such an all-inclusive definition, however, misses the variety of forms, styles and voices which "dramatic monologues" take, especially the multiple views of "monologue" a collection like this reveals. Our own preference, following *Victorian Poetry* (vol. 18, no. 2), is to designate the range of poems included here as "dramatic 'I' poems." This phrase finally proves more useful than the popular but monolithic "dramatic monologue" since it allows discussion of how both the "drama" and the "I" of the poems are constructed.

Traditionally there are two ways of talking about dramatic "I" poems. The first has concerned itself with the historic and formal developments of the poems as genre. Alan Sinfield's *Dramatic Monologue* provides a neat summary of this view. Dating the use of a dramatic "I" to Greek oratory and Quintillian's emphasis upon *prosopopoeia*, the assumption of another's voice and viewpoint (Sinfield 1977: 42), Sinfield sees historic continuity within dramatic "I" works. More importantly, he maintains that dramatic "I" poems fell into three primary genres – the epistle, the complaint and the humorous monologue – until well into the eighteenth century (Sinfield 1977: 42–52). A glance at our contents list shows how true this generalization is: Pope's "Eloisa to Abelard," Leapor's "Strephon to Celia. A Modern Love-Letter"; Dryden's "Farewell, Ungrateful Traitor"; Behn's "Sylvio's Complaint: A Song, To a Fine Scotch Tune"; Chaucer's "Prologe of the Wyves Tale of Bathe." Understanding the forms such dramatic "I" poems initially took, we may see connections with the later works anthologized here, connections which readings of cross-gendered verse will only enhance.

The dramatic monologue has been defined as a dramatic "I" poem which includes the presence of a silent listener, or internal auditor. Cross-gendered poetry, however, undermines such a distinction. The very act of writing across gender is inherently dramatic and, as such, needs no auditor for the the poem to be a "performance." Regardless of whether an auditor – of whatever gender – is present, crossing gender dramatizes social relations. In the end, to pigeonhole a cross-gendered poem as either a dramatic monologue or lyric ignores exactly how a cross-gendered poem resists these categories.

Understanding the poem as a psychological venue constitutes a second tradition of reading the dramatic "I." Here the drama established by the genre – who is complaining to whom and why? what is the nature of the letter? why a song? – is less important than the psychology of the poem's speaker. Accordingly, our understanding shifts: we remember Browning's "Porphyria's Lover" not because of the *ababb* rhyme scheme but because of the gripping, suspenseful and finally horrifying vision of homicidal madness presented. No genre genealogy could prepare us for the particular shock of and madness in Browning's poem. Instead, a psychological reading defines the poetry based on the complex nature of the "I" itself.

To understand this "I" better, it is useful to employ the notion of the "feint," a term derived from Kate Hamburger's discussion of fictional narrators.[2] For our purposes, a "feint" is the speaker of the poem; it is the "I" itself. Practically, however, the "feint" marks a fluid, shifting relationship between poet and "I"/speaker. The notion of the feint denies any direct equivalence between the poet writing and the "I" speaking, allowing us to read the "I" in relation to, but not *as*, the poet. Rather than being unique, there are many possible feints existing on a continuum, sliding along a register between two poles. At one end is a feint which equates poet and speaker while at the other

[196]

is a feint which dissociates poet from speaker. For example, the feint of "Tintern Abbey" by William Wordsworth would represent one end of the scale – "I" as poet – and the feint of the "Prologe of the Wyves Tale of Bathe" the other – "I" as fictionalized character. The placement of a particular feint along the register is therefore a function of the relation between poet and speaker.

Other criticism, however, has noted at least four types of poems which can be characterized by their feints' fixed place on the continuum. In particular, Robert Langbaum and Ralph Rader have delineated the possible forms taken by dramatic "I" poems. Langbaum's founding contribution to this inquiry was his recognition that "dramatic monologue" was not a unified category since we can identify at least one other kind of dramatic "I" poem. Rereading the presence of the Romantic poet in the poet's own lyrics as dramatic, Langbaum coined the phrase "dramatic lyric" to differentiate the Romantic trope from the character-based dramatic monologues of the Victorians. In "The Dramatic Monologue and Related Lyric Forms," Rader refined this idea to include a distinction based on our perception of speakers within the two sorts of poems. He insisted that in dramatic monologues we experience the "I" as we would experience the Other, replete with its own specific situation and personality. Consequently, we watch as well as listen to the "I" delivering its lines during the course of the poem. For instance, our experience of "Porphyria's Lover" is both to hear and see the lover's tale of his room, Porphyria's entrance, ministrations and murder, and his mad afterglow. By witnessing the disjunction between Porphyria's actions and the speaker's interpretations of them – something only possible if we see the actions whole and not solely through his eyes – we understand how unwarranted Porphyria's death is.

"Dramatic lyric," in contrast, depends on a two-fold identification process, primarily limiting our experience to that of the speaker him or herself. In Langbaum's view, the dramatic lyric asks that we identify the poem's "I" with its poet. Rader suggests, however, that the dramatic lyric feint cannot create such perfect identification because readers can only experience a dramatic lyric if they see through the speaker's eyes, mouthing the words along with him or her. Thus a defining characteristic of the dramatic lyric is that the "I" must allow room for readers to participate imaginatively in the retelling of the moment. We may watch Porphyria and her lover from the outside but we *become* Amy Levy's grieving lover in "In the Mile End Road," a connection which creates the poem's success.

Rader subsequently claimed to double the types of identifiable dramatic "I" poems. By rereading Langbaum's work on Wordsworth, Rader derived the notion of the "expressive lyric," in which we *must* identify speaker with author. "Tintern Abbey," for example, could only be spoken by Wordsworth; his is the only combination of situation and personality, or "subjectivity," which makes sense for that specific "I." The feint in this type of poem is thus opposed to the dramatic monologue's fictionalized "I," beyond even a dramatic lyric feint which suggests we identify the speaker with the poet. Finally, Rader delineated the "mask lyric" in which part of the poet's subjectivity is expressed (or suppressed) via a named third-person persona. Figures such as Eliot's Prufrock and Tennyson's Ulysses find their place here, their feints occupying the continuum's formal middle-ground.

The more we worked to gather and think about the poems of this anthology, however, the more we realized that these four categories – dramatic monologue, dramatic lyric, expressive lyric, and mask lyric – did not adequately describe the poetry collected. (Especially since neither Rader nor Langbaum consider gender or the crossing of gender in their analyses.) We sought a term applicable to any genre of poem while still descriptive of the "I" speaking all of the poetry: we arrived at "cross-gendered verse." Our understanding of cross-gendered poems is that they work as a meshing of mask and dramatic lyric, regardless of whether their genre itself is lyrical. That is, the "I" which speaks most of these poems operates somewhere between the named mask and the anonymous "I" who is aligned with its poet. (Saying this is to acknowledge that poems such as Donne's "Sapho to Philaenis," Pope's "Eloisa to Abelard," Swinburne's "Anactoria," and Bidart's "Ellen West" act as more overt, though still complex, mask lyrics.) Whether the speaker is named or not – given an Other's subjectivity or not – the very act of writing the other gender allows the poet to express a part of her or his own subjectivity often unwritten otherwise. Gender-crossing acts as a mask even while the poem, with that "I" which invites our participation in the retelling, may have more in common with a dramatic lyric.

Understanding the cross-gendered poem this way is to see it not only as a new form of verse, but also as an argument against biological essentialism. Cross-gendered poems refuse to acknowledge that gender is determined (and has been historically determined) on the basis of biology, where men and women are gendered solely because of their various reproductive organs. If the genders are *essentially* different, then no real empathy for another gender could be produced and no successful cross-gendered poems could exist. However, following Rader's notion that masks "express and delimit a *personal* emotion" (Rader 1984: 106, our emphasis), then the emotion projected onto an other-gendered speaker must find its root in the poet him or herself. The cross-gendered "I" at once projects part of the poet's subjectivity even as it portrays someone different from the poet. Such a gesture across gender shows precisely the empathy which essentialism would deny: the ability of one gendered subjectivity to act upon and shape another conscientiously. Having begun with the complicated poetic issues of the speaking "I" and its relationship to the poet, then, we arrive at a discussion of the twinned literary questions of "subjectivity" and "agency."

## Rewriting Crusoe: subjectivity and agency in poetry

Fundamentally, the "subject" of a poem is not the poem's content but the speaking "I" within the poem who acts and is acted upon. Within the poem's world, these simultaneous and dialectical acts are ever-shifting, as the degree to which the speaker determines her or his behavior varies. Consequently, literary theorists discuss "subject positions," where a poem's "subject" is often understood as the fluctuating sum of her or his subject positions. For us, the opening lines of Elizabeth Bishop's "Crusoe in England" provide a pointed example of how such positions arise and circumscribe the poet's cross-gendered subject.

The poem begins with Crusoe recounting a newspaper story about the discovery of a named volcano on an island not his own. He is speaking about reading; the "I" shifts from what the papers say to another indeterminate moment, when "last week I was reading/ where some ship saw an island being born." As memory moves within these lines, both ship and island become personified, and the inanimate comes to life. However, in narrating these events, the "I" also details a life in England that has rendered him a reader rather than a doer. Nor can he name: where once Crusoe was an Adam, now he knows "my poor old island's still/un-rediscovered, un-renamable." In this stanza while Crusoe speaks, implicit others – the papers, They, and ultimately "the books" – dominate the field of action. The "I" is our subject, a Crusoe who narrates and dictates the events of the poem, but he is also defined for us by those very events *as they are narrated*, his subject-position ever-changing.

This stanza's "I" never actually tells, he only retells from a story read last week. This incapacity indicates a breakdown of agency, the subject's failure to generate a narrative, or to act and change his own life. He has become his own history, a man remembered, an artifact. Later in the poem when loneliness deepens into existential grief – "Now I live here, another island,/ that doesn't seem like one, but who decides?" – the "I" succumbs to a life in England amidst dead things. Crusoe has become a man of rote, his prior accomplishments rotting, the once amazing parasol now "like a plucked and skinny fowl." Agency is compromised here since for this "I" retelling does not mean re-inventing.

It is Crusoe's effort to assert agency – to "rename" and "rediscover" – which allows Bishop to rewrite literary history in "Crusoe in England." Likewise, the dual project of "renaming" and "rediscovering" reminds the contemporary reader of the various feminist efforts to deconstruct, appropriate, or otherwise rename the male world as they (re)discover "history," "philosophy," etc. To experience Bishop's Crusoe is thus to engage a larger effort historically removed from Defoe's literary character. In this view, reading the subjectivity of a cross-gendered poem's speaker is always at least partially dependent upon understanding its cross-gendered creation: indeed, to read a speaker's identity here is to read gender itself.

## Reading gender in cross-gendered verse

To say that we must read gender in order to read cross-gendered verse is to acknowledge that – no matter the subject positions, plot, themes, or "point" of the poems – "gender" is also always a topic of the cross-gendered poem. "Gender," however, is often defined in conflicting ways within every area of contemporary criticism: feminism (whether Anglo-American, French, post-colonial, activist, radical); men's studies; Queer

Theory; and the multiple disciplines – history, literature, sociology, biology, philosophy – which come together as gender studies.[3] In our reading, a distinction between "gender" and the more familiar and colloquial "sex" is fundamental.

Following a long-standing tradition in gender studies, we understand "sex" to be a biological happenstance and "gender" to be a culturally determined field. "Sex" makes a mass of tissue; "gender" makes the mass a culturally recognizable and thus readable body. When the new-born child is presented to its proud parents, they ask "What is it – girl or boy?" Even before any response is given, they read the pink cap and have their answer. This body is read as all bodies are, within the codes – pink for girls, blue for boys – and categories – female, male – which society provides. As we all do hundreds of times daily, the parents fix a gender to the body before them.[4] Though a body may have a sex determined genitally, chromosomally or hormonally, it is gender which we read onto it time and again.

If "sex" is what one "has" or "is" and "gender" is not biologically determined, then it makes sense that gender is performed, something one does. As a result, the social performance and interpretation of gender relies upon markers such as clothes, sex, sexual practice and desire. To read people walking down the street is to read the gendered clues – clothes, gait, bearing, grooming, etc. – which they have prepared, marked themselves with, done. We decisively gender-interpret their bodies, even without recourse to sexual practice or insight into their desires. Reading a literary subject's identity is much the same: we read textual markers and fit them into the received cultural categories – man, woman, masculine, feminine – we mostly presume.

The flaw in this summary, however, comes precisely in the dual nature of the categories themselves. The common take on gender is that it mimics biological dimorphism: there are two genders, male and female, just as there are two biologically determined sexes.[5] However, gender need *not* appear in only two forms (the male/female binary) if gender itself is a culturally determined label based on sex, the performance of sexual acts, and the projection of desire – practices which will shift moment-to-moment within every subjectivity. As critical theory has argued, the very form of the binary creates a superior and inferior division; as feminist theorists among others have shown, this division has favored the male in Western culture. Indeed, it is by now well-noted that the male/female binary is strongly connected to those other hierarchies perpetuated and incorporated by Western society: male/female = mind/body, rational/irrational, universal/particular, invisible/visible, dominant/submissive, subject/object.

What happens, though, if the body we read does not conform to these gender assumptions? Looking at transvestites, for instance, Marjorie Garber contends that the clothes do *not* make the man. Instead, the unreadability of the transvestite – effeminate man? masculine woman? none of the above? – provides a site where the binary of gender is broken; a "third term" is introduced. Our proposal is that cross-gendering also creates a "third term," another way of conceiving gender. Cross-gendered verse may escape the dualism of "male" and "female" subjectivity because the poem's "I" is never fully embodied, male or female. It is rather a blending of the two, a place which demands refining our suppositions regarding gender.

Each cross-gendered poem does not necessarily do this, however. Some may actually perpetuate more conventional notions of gender. Thus Chaucer's powerful and vocal Wife of Bath inverts the dominant/submissive binary. However, her concern with sexual bodies and sexuality itself reinforces "woman's" link to the body just as her misprisions of Scripture dramatize irrationality; any reading of her must end with talking about who she is rather than what she says. Likewise, drawing on the same disjunction between spirit and body as the Wife of Bath, Yeats' Crazy Jane ends up reinforcing gender hierarchies. She, too, is unable or unwilling to forgo the body and, instead, elevates it to one of the eternal things which "remain in God." Even here, however, gender is constructed along the lines of the stereotypical notions of the woman who waits behind while "men come, men go"; the woman whose body is "all," the well-traversed road; the woman whose access to the world of God, so long the purview of men, is as a body. Although both Jane and the Wife may be strong voices, neither can achieve more than a temporary inversion of the hierarchies so strongly linked to gender.

Thus male writers often reinscribe their women narrators into a binary which favors "male" positions. Similarly, women poets often use male narrators who, through speech or subject position (or both), echo a concern with finding a language and place of their own. To chart a brief line here, we begin with Aphra Behn's loving swain in "The Dream." Although he seems to narrate a vision of the disembodied (and almost dismembered) female love-object, Aminta, Behn's over-writing here – "trembling," "bliss," "rapture," "resistance," "heaven of my desires," "nimbler motions," "height of languishment," "new charms," "last mystery of Love" – undercuts the male, and female, positions. In essence, the poet's own subjectivity shines through her ironic portrayal of her male speaker. Elizabeth Barrett Browning's "A Man's Requirements" accomplishes a similar result. Her speaker finally undermines the devotion we might have seen in him after twenty stanzas enumerating the physical and emotional elements with which his "dear" ought to love him:

> Thus, if thou wilt prove me, dear,
> Woman's love no fable,
> *I* will love *thee* – half a year –
> As a man is able.

Echoing Pluto's abduction of Proserpine, the "I" is cast ironically as at once fickle and threatening.

May Swenson's use of a male speaker in "First Walk on the Moon" emphasizes the Apollo 11 astronauts' inability to characterize their environment accurately. Like so many contemporary feminist critics, they struggle to find names not already co-opted by another's discourse. Swenson's solution, using quotation marks to frame the linguistically imprecise, reminds us of the French post-structuralist use of words *sous rature*, or under erasure: we must use these words because they are the only ones we have, but they are used under erasure because they still do not convey the precise meanings we intend or find. Finally, Suniti Namjoshi's use of Caliban echoes both feminist and post-colonial responses to gender issues. As the colonized native, Caliban struggles toward knowledge, acceptance and a world "populated" by "nice people" unlike those he encounters as the subject of Prospero and Miranda's (and Shakespeare's) control.

Reading how cross-gendered poems have allowed men and women to underscore their own relationships to gender, however, says little of that "third" possibility latent in the form itself: what might this "third term" look like in a cross-gendered poem? One possibility is presented in Frank Bidart's "Ellen West" as his anorectic narrator attempts to "*defeat* 'Nature'" by starving herself. Understood as a social disorder, anorexia may be seen as an extreme instance of encoding, in which a culture's expectations are inscribed onto a body – and, as we know, anorexia's bodies are almost always female. Bidart refashions Ellen West's anorexia as an individual *spiritual* crisis, however, effectively rewriting Chaucer's body/spirit split rather than creating just another "mad" narrator. In the process, he rewrites the gender assumptions perpetuated by the canon.

Quite simply, Ellen does not just want to thin down her body; she wants to abandon it altogether, to become one whose "body is the image of her soul":

The ideal of being thin

conceals the ideal
*not* to have a body – ;

which is *NOT* trivial.

This absent body, this soul, is what Ellen labels "her true self," a concept reminiscent of sociology's "depth body." Ellen reads two bodies throughout the poem: there is the physical body which she decimates daily, inscribes with the marks of anorexia, but there is also that "depth body," the internal and sustained image, which is unmarked and which nourishes her. If "the 'modern body' is read symptomatically, in terms of what it hides" (Grosz 1990: 69), then reading Ellen West reveals her deeper desire to overcome the body in order to be the soul.

As Ellen indicates, though, the body is not that easily discarded. Even she admits that it has its uses: "without a body, who can/*know* himself at all?" Yet Ellen's knowledge, although relentlessly carnal, delights in the denial of the body. Emblematically, the verbs which characterize her existence are "acting; choosing; rejecting" – or, as she puts it at the poem's end, "refusing." Ellen ultimately rejects the body itself and the world for which it stands by denying her body its sustenance, letting her "tapeworm . . . soul" consume her body altogether.

The stakes of this refusal are obviously high for her, but they are equally high for our reading of her. In Ellen's formulation we can see the dialectic of body and spirit. Wondering about Maria Callas' own "soul," Ellen asks "Is *it* bitter?" (our emphasis). Neither male nor female and more than simply an inverted male subjectivity, this "it" is outside the realm of a Western dualism always tied so strongly to bodies:

[204]

                                                    This *I* is anterior

to name; gender; action;
fashion;

                    MATTER ITSELF . . .

The "I" she seeks, that depth body, that soul, is one unbound by the
codes read onto the body, including those of gendered subjectivity
("name; gender" and "fashion") and agency ("action," even "rejecting"
and "refusing"). Within the poem, then, the "soul" becomes the
third term which Bidart develops as a way to question gender and its
bodies.

There is also a larger issue of gender construction inherent in Bidart's
writing Ellen at all. When Ellen interprets the people around her, the
people on her train ride home for instance, she projects her discomfort
with her own body onto their relationships with their bodies. Her
interpretation is limited by her own concerns. Recalling our earlier
discussion of the cross-gendered feint, we might say that Bidart's writing
is similarly projective. Because of his own concerns, Ellen becomes
his narrator and "soul" his third term. This is not to limit the
poem's achievement, but to acknowledge that, within cross-gendered
poetry, Ellen West is always partially Frank Bidart just as Frank Bidart
is necessarily partially Ellen West. The very act of reading a cross-
gendered poem blurs gender distinctions and subverts the gender
binary. When the poems of this anthology are combined in different
ways it may be seen that the cross-gendered poem subverts other
conventions and suppositions.

## Supplementing gender: other reading trajectories

On one level, poetry has always been an art engaged in conversation
with and about itself: because every word contains its past, every new
poem enters into a dialogue with previous poems. As a result, the
formal and prosodic achievements of a particular era should be understood not only as specific to their moment but also as a rereading of
history. Each new poem proves a lens through which the past is viewed
differently. This way of reading is especially relevant to the history of
cross-gendered verse, just as it is relevant to the student attempting

an historically-based examination of the poems anthologized here. As formal concerns become literary phenomena and thematic coincidences become genre, the reader begins to see more than just the present in the contemporary – and to realize how, for instance, Yusef Komunyakaa's "The Thorn Merchant's Mistress" might become a dialogue with Sir Walter Ralegh's "The Nymph's Reply to the Shepherd."

This is not to say, however, that Komunyakaa has responded specifically to Ralegh, or that any sub-grouping of the works here might be considered an argument for the cross-gendered poem as either tradition or canon. Yet the early pages of the anthology are rife with pastorals, just as the latter pages present variations on social concerns – and such literary coincidences have always warranted further examination. (Of course, despite an editorial commitment to balance and quality, the contents of the volume have also been shaped, an argument by praxis, and further informed by the collaborative judgment of two male editors.) With all of these protestations in mind we offer the following avenues for future travel, ways and byways to read these poems together.

Although vestiges persist, no pastoral poems appear among the contemporary works collected here, since the genre is, by and large, of the past. Like the ballad, the pastoral was long the home to colloquialisms set against a rural or rustic background, but unlike the ballad, the idealized and stereotyped values of the pastoral reached their zenith (or nadir) in the rococo, and became less and less connected to life. And yet, the presence here of Robert Greene's "The Shepherd's Wife's Song" and the naiveté with which the speaker extols the swain's carefree existence set a stage for later poems – and the use, by poets of the early nineteenth century, of colloquial realism as a conscious subversion of the pastoral.

In the work of the Victorian poets, the colloquial was often employed as a measure of class. Yet the cross-gendered poem had concomitantly become an instrument of social and political reform in the name of the co-opted class. As African-American poets such as Priscilla Jane Thompson and, later, Langston Hughes began to write race in terms of a folk and oral tradition, the colloquial arose as a linguistic means to self-determination. In more recent works, in the poems of Gwendolyn Brooks and Lucille Clifton, the language itself, as well as the ideas of "passing" and hegemony, become subjects for the poem;

as Clifton suggests in the voice of the Los Angeles policeman who beat Rodney King, the "nations of darkness/ speaking a language i do not understand" contribute to a bigot's rage. Finally, in Ai's horrific vision of the 1981 Atlanta child-killer, we are given a psychopathology imbued with a warped ethic, "work, work for the joy of it" as well as "the black boys/ who know too much,/ but not enough to stay away." The violent collision of cultures in Ai's poem, of the oral tradition and the last two lines' iambs, and of references to Saturn and the Good Shepherd, reiterate the character's physical violence. Although no one would argue that this poem descends from the pastoral, we find in its meaning-making a linguistic historicism which can only make us see the pastoral differently.

The cross-gendered poem has not accidentally become a place for African-American women to explore the linguistic ground of white and/or male violence, since the cross-gendered poet often writes the unwritten. In a similar vein, what might seem coy sexual banter may be translated into highly charged sexual allegory within the symbolic venue of the cross-gendered poem. The poses of the subject manifest a sexuality of startling resonance, from Chaucer's "Prologe of the Wyves Tale of Bathe" through the epistolary reversals of Pope's "Eloisa to Abelard" and Judith Madan's "Abelard to Eloisa"; from Browning and Barrett Browning's correspondence in "A Woman's Last Word" and "A Man's Requirements" to Adrienne Rich's "The Loser" and Michael Heffernan's "The Message."

The contents pages of this book document the cross-gendered poem as social history. There is a wealth of "mad poems" here, and the phenomenon of men writing women *in this way* provides a short history of sexism – until the roles are reversed and/or subverted in the recent poems of Lucille Clifton, Richard Howard, Heather McHugh and Ai. Additionally, and not incidentally, even the choice of speaker in the contemporary cross-gendered poem reveals a widespread discomfiture with conventionally gendered roles, as seen in Auden's Miranda, Ashbery's Empress, and Hughes' Cleopatra; as well as Rukeyser's George Robinson, Rich's Loser and Namjoshi's Caliban.

It is not surprising that so many songs appear in the early works anthologized here – including the poems of Breton, Lodge, Herrick, Wroth, Blake, Burns and Baillie. The absence of the song from the latter half of this volume, however, deserves investigation. With the exception of W. H. Auden's villanelle, no closed-form songs appear within the poems of the twentieth century, although the anthology certainly includes its share of recent formal verse. This lack of interest in the song stands as a consequence of the Victorians' success in the dramatic monologue and lyric, and proves further that the ascendancy of Browning, Tennyson, among others has altered irrevocably how poets perceive the cross-gendered poem.

Auden's song, however, also brings to light the dramatization of high art/low art aesthetic concerns, especially when read adjacent to and against the volume's only other twentieth-century song, Muriel Rukeyser's "George Robinson: Blues." Itself a part of a much longer dramatic poem, a reworking of *The Tempest*, Auden's villanelle aspires to a classical condition of music beautifully – just as Rukeyser aims elsewhere, employing an indigenous American form, the blues, as she crosses race in addition to gender. Both poems know whence they come; both poems present their concerns precisely and gracefully. Whereas Auden's revision of *The Tempest* affirms an art defined by literature, a metaphorical reworking of earlier metaphor, Rukeyser's metonymies explore an art defined by experience.

These aesthetic issues – art and experience – lead to a discussion of the purpose of art and thus quite naturally to politics and the cross-gendered poem. Given the intimacy of the speaking subject in these works, and how the feint often achieves the appearance of a confession, when the cross-gendered poet takes on political issues she or he often appears to do so on necessarily personal terms. In Tennyson's "Rizpah," for example, the consequences of what may be a son's brutish crime become questioned if not questionable; the "I" evinces our sympathy, a mother whose actions against an unfeeling judicial system recall Antigone. In more recent verse, the cross-gendered poem has remained a powerful forum for political ideas especially as prior notions of the political poem have become subsumed within the "poetry of witness," where writers seek to record atrocities as protest. However in contemporary cross-gendered verse, political issues are often explored empathetically instead of sympathetically.

Rather than have a speaker testify to unseen evil and thus inspire sympathetic rage from a reader who also knows better, contemporary poets seem to prefer a cross-gendered "I" with a terrible past who has personally committed crimes. Here, the reader is asked to empathize with the "I," to love thine enemy while never quite forgiving her or his behavior. In both Clifton's "powell" and Ai's "The Good Shepherd:

Atlanta 1981" we see this phenomenon, evil ventriloquated in an attempt to understand its origins. Such an approach has historical and literary precedent – in Milton's Satan, for example, among other anti-heroes – but the prevalence of this empathetic act within contemporary cross-gendered verse is remarkable. As it stands, the twentieth century cross-gendered political poem is more likely to perform villainy than victimization.

For both the teacher and student of creative writing reading this volume – not for what the poems mean but how, not to historicize but to borrow – the works collected here exemplify various approaches to the fundamental problem of character development and credibility. As a result, careful study of the linguistic devices, narrative poses and formal stratagems which combine to establish a dramatic "I" yields significant information. If, as John Hollander has said of Richard Howard's monologues, the poems here may be considered "personations" rather than fictions (Hollander 1994: 7), such close reading could prove central to a student poet's own work with character. This work would reveal how successful crossing of gender may be seen as exemplar of the well-realized Other. (Moreover, such analysis would also prove enlightening in terms of its ventriloquations, especially for those students and teachers in Performance Studies.)

## Some conclusions: understanding the place of cross-gendered verse

Every major English-language literary movement of the past five centuries has given us cross-gendered poems of note. However, to attempt a generalist's perspective and view this poetic phenomenon as canonical is to rekindle questions which already inflame current literary debate. Many contemporary writers have undertaken the task of revisionism: reconsideration of male mythologies and cultural conventions underscores feminist projects everywhere. But to suggest that the cross-gendered poem has been an active part of these projects is to position the present at the expense of history. For example, a startling abundance of feminist myth-making may be found within this anthology, a confluence of aesthetics and concerns which answers the work of the Victorian poets – that is, mostly the work of men in a culture dominated by men. Until the cross-gendered poem achieves status as either a movement or a genre, however, the contemporary revisionist poems should be seen as parallel to the canon, apart from the whole; poets today are not yet writing cross-gendered verse in response to other cross-gendered verse, and certainly not in the way the Victorians wrote to and for each other.

Has there been a resurgence of the cross-gendered poem? Is the cross-gendered poem enjoying a period of significant achievement? Rather marvelously, neither of these questions seems relevant given the contents of this volume – for if a phenomenon never abates, it need not be revitalized. What this volume does let us question, though, is the historical relationship between gender and poetry, and how sexism perpetuates its own assumptions – and, accordingly to discover in the contemporary such transcendent poetic gestures as the "third term." The value of this book, then, lies in its subject: in the symbolic venue of the cross-gendered poem, we find the Other, and thus ourselves.

## Notes

1  Personal telephone conversation, January 1995.
2  The "feint" is also developed in Sinfield's *Dramatic Monologue* (cf. pp. 25, ff.). Our use of the concept expands upon his by presenting its application to the formal and psychological categories developed by Richard Langbaum and Ralph W. Rader.
3  This is to say nothing of the multiple takes on gender which occurred before and after structuralism. For a particularly useful discussion of these differences see Judith Butler's *Gender Trouble*; her first chapter's reading of Michel Foucault, Luce Irigaray and Monique Wittig alongside Simone de Beauvoir elegantly sums up the various positions.
4  The pink/blue contrast was not always interpreted as it is today; earlier in the century, the gender connections for the two colors were reversed. See Marjorie Garber's discussion in *Vested Interests*, pp. 1–2.
5  John Money's thirty years of research into the biology of sex has shown that "sex" is actually polymorphic in more instances than we might imagine. His collection of papers, *Venuses Penuses*, is a useful reminder that even "sex" is necessarily open to cultural interpretation.

# Selected Bibliographies

Neither exhaustive nor definitive, the bibliographies below are intended to suggest further reading in diverse areas, supplementing study of issues raised by our essay. As such, we have purposefully included a large number of essay collections which address topics from several viewpoints; we have also endeavored to include books by single authors which students might find more easily than they would articles in professional journals.

## The dramatic monologue and dramatic "I" poems

ABRAMS, M. H. (1965) "Structure and Style in the Greater Romantic Lyric," in F. W. Hilles and H. Bloom (eds) *From Sensibility to Romanticism: Essay Presented to Frederick A. Pottle*, New York: Oxford University Press.

CULLER, D. (1975) "Monodrama and the Dramatic Monologue," *PMLA* 90: 366–85.

CULLER, J. (1977) "Apostrophe," *Diacritics* 7: 59–69.

ELIOT, T. S. (1973) "The Three Voices of Poetry," *Poetry and Poets*, 10th edition, New York: The Noonday Press.

—— (1980) *The Use of Poetry and the Use of Criticism*, London: Faber & Faber.

FAAS, K. E. (1970) "Notes towards a History of the Dramatic Monologue," *Anglia* 88: 222–32.

FUSON, B. (1948) *Browning and His English Predecessors in the Dramatic Monolog*, State University of Iowa Humanistic Studies VIII, Iowa City: State University of Iowa.

GARRATT, R. (1973) "Browning's Dramatic Monologue: The Strategy of the Double Mask," *Victorian Poetry* 11: 115–25.

HAMBURGER, K. (1973) *The Logic of Literature*, Bloomington: Indiana University Press.

HARRIS, D. (1982) "The 'Figured Page': Dramatic Epistle in Browning and Yeats," in Richard J. Finneran (ed.) *Yeats Annual* 1: 1333–94.

—— (1984) "D. G. Rossetti's 'Jenny': Sex, Money, and the Interior Monologue," *Victorian Poetry* 22: 197–216.

HARTY, E. R. (1990) "Voice and Enunciation in the Dramatic Monologue and the Lyric," *Unisa English Studies* 28, 1: 14–21.

HOBSBAUM, P. (1975) "The Rise of the Dramatic Monologue," *Hudson Review* 28: 228–45.

JONES, A. R. (1967) "Robert Browning and the Dramatic Monologue: The Impersonal Art," *Critical Quarterly* 9: 301–28.

LANGBAUM, R. (1957) *The Poetry of Experience: The Dramatic Monologue in Modern Literary Tradition*, Chicago: University of Chicago Press.

MARTIN, L. (1979) "The Inside of Time: An Essay on the Dramatic Monologue," in H. Bloom and A. Munich (eds) *Robert Browning: A Collection of Critical Essays*, Englewood Cliffs, NJ: Prentice Hall.

—— (1985) *Browning's Dramatic Monologues and the Post-Romantic Subject*, Baltimore: Johns Hopkins University Press.

MERMIN, D. (1983) *The Audience in the Poem*, New Brunswick: Rutgers University Press.

RADER, R. (1976) "The Dramatic Monologue and Related Lyric Forms," *Critical Inquiry* 3: 131–51.

—— (1984) "Notes on Some Structural Varieties and Variations in Dramatic 'I' Poems and Their Theoretical Implications," *Victorian Poetry* 22: 103–20.

ROGERS, W. (1983) *Three Genres and the Interpretations of Lyric*, Princeton: Princeton University Press.

SESSIONS, I. (1947) "The Dramatic Monologue," *PMLA* 62: 503–16.

SHAW, W. D. (1979) "Victorian Poetry and Repression: The Use and Abuse of Masks," *English Literary History* 46: 468–94.

SINFIELD, A. (1977) *Dramatic Monologue*, London: Methuen.

TUCKER, H. (1984) "From Monomania to Monologue: 'St. Simeon Stylites' and the Rise of Victorian Dramatic Monologue," *Victorian Poetry* 22: 121–38.

—— (1986) "Dramatic Monologue and the Overhearing of Lyric," in C. Hosek and P. Parker (eds) *Lyric Poetry: Beyond New Criticism*, Ithaca: Cornell University Press.

## Gender and literary studies

ABEL, E. (ed.) (1980) *Writing and Sexual Difference*, Chicago: University of Chicago Press.

ABEL, E. and ABEL, E. (eds) (1983) *The Signs Reader: Women, Gender and Scholarship*, Chicago, University of Chicago Press.

BAKHTIN, M. M. (1981) "Discourse in The Novel," in *The Dialogic Imagination*, trans. C. Emerson and M. Holquist, Austin: University of Texas Press.

BAL, M. "The Rhetoric of Subjectivity," *Poetics Today* 5, 2: 337–76.

BIRKERTS, S. (1987) *An Artificial Wilderness: Essays on Twentieth Century Literature*, New York: William & Morrow.

BROWN, C. and OLSEN, K. (eds) (1978) *Feminist Criticism: Essays on Theory, Poetry, and Prose*, Metuchen, NJ: Scarecrow Press.

CLARIDGE, L. and LANGLAND, E. (eds) (1990) *Out of Bounds: Male Writers and Gender(ed) Criticism*, Amherst: University of Massachusetts Press.

DOLLIMORE, J. (1991) *Sexual Dissidence: Augustine to Wilde, Freud to Foucault*, Oxford: Clarendon Press.

DUPLESSIS, R. B. (1990) *The Pink Guitar: Writing as Feminist Practice*, New York: Routledge.

FUSS, D. (1991) *Inside/Out: Lesbian Theories, Gay Theories*, New York: Routledge.

GALLOP, J. (1982) *The Daughter's Seduction: Feminism and Psychoanalysis*, Ithaca: Cornell University Press.

GILBERT, S. M. and GUBAR, S. (1979a) *The Madwoman in the Attic: The Woman Writer and the Nineteenth-Century Literary Imagination*, New Haven: Yale University Press.

—— (1979b) *Shakespeare's Sisters: Feminist Essays on Women Poets*, Bloomington: Indiana University Press.

—— (1989) *No Man's Land, Vol. 2. Sexchanges*, New Haven: Yale University Press.

HEILBRUN, C. G. (1979) *Reinventing Womanhood*, New York: W. W. Norton.

HOLLANDER, J. (1994) "Introduction to Richard Howard's Marie Bullock Poetry Reading," *Poetry Pilot* Winter 1994–5: 7–8.

IRONS, G. (ed.) (1992) *Gender, Language, and Myth: Essays on Popular Narrative*, Toronto: University of Toronto Press.

JACOBUS, M. (1986) *Reading Woman: Essays in Feminist Criticism*, New York: Columbia University Press.

JONES, R. (ed.) (1985) *Poetry and Politics: An Anthology of Essays*, New York: Quill.

LANGLAND, E. (1990) "Images of Women: A Literature Perspective," in M. A. Paludi and G. A. Steuernagel (eds) *Foundations for a Feminist Restructuring of the Academic Disciplines*, New York: Haworth Press.

MILLET, K. (1970) *Sexual Politics*, New York: Doubleday.

MOI, T. (1985) *Sexual/Textual Politics: Feminist Literary Theory*, New York: Methuen.

MORGAN, T. (ed.) (1994) *Men Writing the Feminine: Literature, Theory, and the Question of Genders*, Albany: State University of New York Press.

OSTRIKER, A. (1983) *Writing Like A Woman*, Ann Arbor: University of Michigan Press.

ROSE, J. (1986) *Sexuality in the Field of Vision*, London: Verso.

SEDGEWICK, E. K. (1985) *Between Men: English Literature and Homosocial Desire*, New York: Columbia University Press.

SHOWALTER, E. (ed.) (1989) *Speaking of Gender*, New York: Routledge.
SILVERMAN, K. (1992) *Male Subjectivity at the Margins*, New York: Routledge.
SONTAG, S. (1966) *Against Interpretation*, New York: Farrar, Straus, & Giroux.
STIMPSON, C. (1988) *Where the Meanings Are: Feminism and Cultural Spaces*, New York: Methuen.
TODD, J. M. (1981) *Men by Women*, New York: Holmes & Meier.

## Gender and the social sciences

ACKROYD, P. (1979) *Dressing Up*, New York: Simon & Schuster.
BUTLER, J. and SCOTT, J. W. (eds) (1992) *Feminists Theorize the Political*, New York: Routledge.
DE BEAUVOIR, S. (1953) *The Second Sex*, trans. H. M. Parshley, New York: Knopf.
GARBER, M. (1992) *Vested Interests: Cross-Dressing and Cultural Anxiety*, New York: Routledge.
GATENS, M. (1983) "A Critique of the Sex/Gender Distinction," in J. Allen and P. Patton (eds) *Beyond Marx? Interventions after Marx*, Sydney: Intervention Press.
GILMAN, S. L. (1989) *Sexuality: An Illustrated History*, New York: John Wiley & Sons.
GOLDSTEIN, L. (ed.) (1994) *The Male Body: Features, Destinies, Exposures*, Ann Arbor: University of Michigan Press.
GROSZ, E. (1990) "Inscriptions and Body-Maps: Representations and the Corporeal," in T. Threadgold and A. Cranny-Francis (eds) *Feminine, Masculine and Representation*, Sydney: Allen & Unwin.
HOOKS, B. (1984) *Feminist Theory: From Margin to Center*, Boston: South End Press.
HUMM, M. (ed.) (1992) *Modern Feminisms: Political, Literary, Cultural*, New York: Columbia University Press.
JARDINE, A. (1985) *Gynesis: Configurations of Women and Modernity*, Ithaca: Cornell University Press.
JARDINE, A. and SMITH, P. (eds) (1987) *Men in Feminism*, New York: Methuen.
KESSLER, S. J. and MCKENNA, W. (1978) *Gender: An Ethnomethodological Approach*, Chicago: University of Chicago Press.
LEHMAN, P. (1993) *Running Scared: Masculinity and the Representation of the Male Body*, Philadelphia: Temple University Press.
MACCORMACK, C. and STRATHERN, M. (eds) *Nature, Culture and Gender*, New York: Cambridge University Press.
MEAD, M. (1949) *Male and Female, A Study of the Sexes in a Changing World*, New York: Morrow.

MORGAN, D. H. (1992) *Discovering Men*, London: Routledge.

PAGLIA, C. (1990) *Sexual Personae: Art and Decadence from Nefertiti to Emily Dickinson*, New Haven: Yale University Press.

PARKER, A., RUSSO, M., SOMMER, D. and YAEGER, P. (eds) (1992) *Nationalisms and Sexualities*, New York: Routledge.

REITER, R. R. (1975) *Toward an Anthropology of Women*, New York: Monthly Review Press.

RICH, A. (1986) "Compulsory Heterosexuality and Lesbian Existence," in *Blood, Bread, and Poetry: Selected Prose 1979–1985*, New York: W. W. Norton.

RILEY, D. (1988) *Am I That Name?: Feminism and the Category of "Women" in History*, New York: Macmillan.

SCOTT, J. W. (1988) *Gender and the Politics of History*, New York: Columbia University Press.

SNITOW, A., STANSELL, C. and THOMPSON, S. (eds) (1983) *Powers of Desire: The Politics of Sexuality*, New York: Monthly Review Press.

SPIVAK, G. C. (1988) *In Other Worlds: Essays in Cultural Politics*, New York: Routledge.

STOLLER, R. J. (1985) *Observing the Erotic Imagination*, New Haven: Yale University Press.

THREADGOLD, T. and CRANNY-FRANCIS, A. (eds) (1990) *Feminine, Masculine and Representation*, Sydney: Allen & Unwin.

VANCE, C. (ed.) (1984) *Pleasure and Danger: Exploring Female Sexuality*, Boston: Routledge.

WEST, C. and ZIMMERMAN, D. (1991) "Doing Gender," in J. Lorber and S. A. Farrell (eds) *The Social Construction of Gender*, Newbury Park, CA: Sage Publications.

WOODHOUSE, A. (1989) *Fantastic Women: Sex, Gender and Transvestism*, New Brunswick: Rutgers University Press.

## Gender and the biological sciences

BLIER, R. (1984) *Science and Gender: A Critique of Biology and Its Theories on Women*, New York: Pergamon.

FOX-KELLER, E. (1984) *Reflections on Gender and Science*, New Haven: Yale University Press.

HARRAWAY, D. (1989) *Primate Visions*, New York: Routledge.

JORDANOVA, L. (1989) *Sexual Visions: Images of Gender in Science and Medicine Between the Eighteenth and Twentieth Centuries*, Madison: University of Wisconsin Press.

MONEY, J. (1986) *Venuses Penuses: Sexology, Sexosophy and Exigency Theory*, Buffalo, NY: Prometheus Press.

STOLLER, R. J. (1968) *Sex and Gender: On the Development of Masculinity and Femininity*, London: The Hogarth Press.


## Gender and French post-structuralism

BUTLER, J. (1990) *Gender Trouble*, New York: Routledge.

CIXOUS, H. (1976) "The Laugh of the Medusa," trans. K. Cohen and P. Cohen, *Signs* 1, Summer: 875–93.

FOUCAULT, M. (1980) *The History of Sexuality, Volume One, An Introduction*, trans. R. Hurley, New York: Vintage.

IRIGARAY, L. (1985a) *The Sex Which is Not One*, trans. C. Porter with C. Burke, Ithaca: Cornell University Press.

—— (1985b) *Speculum of the Other Woman*, trans. G. C. Gill, Ithaca: Cornell University Press.

KRISTEVA, J. (1984) *Desire in Language, a Semiotic Approach to Literature and Art*, trans. M. Walker, New York: Columbia University Press.

LACAN, J. (1977) "The Signification of the Phallus," in *Ecrits: A Selection*, trans. A. Sheridan, New York: W. W. Norton.

WITTIG, M. (1976) *The Lesbian Body*, trans. P. Owen, New York: Avon.

—— (1992) *The Straight Mind and Other Essays*, Boston: Beacon Press.

Printed in the United States
47591LVS00003BA/45